Forward *by*Degrees

The UNIVERSITY
of PAISLEY
1897-1997

Evelyn Hood

The University of Paisley, 1997.

ISBN 0 904391 45 0 limp edition
        0 904391 50 7 hardback

Published by
The University of Paisley

Printed by
Garthland Print,
Glasgow

Foreword

Sir Robert Easton

I am delighted to have the opportunity to introduce this history of the University of Paisley, written and published as part of the University's Centenary celebrations.

The celebration of the Centenary, and the publication of this history, remind us of the important part that Paisley College of Technology, now the University of Paisley, has played in the life of the town and more widely the West of Scotland throughout the last one hundred years.

That wider area has been emphasised by the University's merger with the former Craigie College and subsequent development of the campus in Ayr. More widely still, the recent Nursing Education contract awarded to the University formalises contact with students throughout south west Scotland.

In addition to the large number of students who have benefited from its courses and moved on to employment in the region, and more widely throughout the world, the College has had an economic and social impact on the development of the town of Paisley. It is also worth pointing out the many and intimate contacts between the College and industrial concerns throughout Scotland which have always been a feature of the history of the institution. That close collaboration is still a very prominent feature of the University of Paisley, a collaboration to the benefit of the University's graduates, its staff, and of the many and varied industrial and commercial enterprises involved.

It is particularly appropriate that the text of this history should, emphasising the role of the University within the larger community, have been written by a well known local author. I hope that Evelyn Hood's text will be read widely, as it deserves, throughout the town of Paisley and its surrounding area, as well as by all those connected with the University in any way.

Sir Robert Easton, CBE DUniv
Chancellor of the University of Paisley

Acknowledgements

I am most grateful to the late Dr David Graham and Mr David McDowall for permission to make use of their theses on Paisley's Technical School/College of Technology.

I would also like to thank Mrs Catherine Howie, William Dodge and Bob McLaughlin for their contributions, Hugh Ferguson, author of *Glasgow School of Art – the History* for information regarding some students and teaching staff in the early part of the twentieth century, all those who agreed to be interviewed for the University's oral history project, and those who, in other ways, contributed information used in this book.

Evelyn Hood

Picture Acknowledgements

The Editor acknowledges the assistance of the following people and organisations who have kindly provided the illustrations used in this book.

Every effort has been made to trace copyright holders and apologies are offered for any unintended oversight.

The Editor is particularly grateful to Alastair Donald of the Educational Development Unit; David Rowand, author of *A Pictorial History of Paisley;* the Mitchell Library, Glasgow and Paisley Museum and Art Galleries, Renfrewshire Council.

Thanks are also due to Jim Adams, Douglas Armour, Sheena Bain, A McGregor Clark, Classic Cards (formerly Valentines of Dundee), Meg Ferguson, Bill Fullarton, *The Herald* and *Evening Times, The Glasgow Illustrated*, Glasgow University Archives and Business Records Centre, Avril Goodwin (Craigie Library), Joseph Kerr, Robert Lees, Adam Lynch, Professor Willie McEwan, Hamish Maclachlan, Sam Paton, John G. Paul, Betty Reid, Department of Medical Illustrations, Royal Infirmary Health Board Trust, Alasdair Russell, Professor Roy Sinclair, Alan Wilson and Dr Jim Wood.

Stuart James

Author's Note

Born and raised in Paisley, I had always been aware of 'the Tech's' existence, but it was only when I began to write this history that I discovered that for the last 100 years an entire community has been living within and parallel to the town of Paisley, with its own fascinating history. I hope that those who read this book will enjoy it as much as I enjoyed writing it.

The University has grown considerably since its humble beginnings, and the task of recording that growth has been far from easy. Some events and stories have had to be set aside in order to make room for others; I can only express my regret over this, and trust that the problems experienced in writing any history are appreciated.

My thanks to the University's Centenary Committee for giving me the opportunity to write the history, to Principal Richard Shaw, Librarian Stuart James and Depute Librarian Gordon McCrae for their support, interest and encouragement, and to my researcher, Alasdair Russell, who dug into the past with such enthusiasm that I almost had to move to a larger house to accommodate the information he uncovered.

Finally, I would also like to express my gratitude to my husband, Jim Hood, for his patience, support and assistance in the writing of the book.

Evelyn Hood

Contents

Abbreviations used in this book

BA	Bachelor of Arts
BAe	British Aerospace
BD	Bachelor of Divinity
BSc	Bachelor of Science
BSc (Eng)	Bachelor of Science (Engineering)
BSI	British Standards Institution
CAD/CAM	Computer Aided Design/Computer Aided Manufacture
CATS	Credit Accumulation and Transfer Scheme
CI	Central Institution
CLIC	Centre for Liaison with Industry and Commerce
CNAA	Council for National Academic Awards
DipTech	Diploma of Technology
DSIR	Department of Scientific and Industrial Research
DTI	Department of Trade and Industry
DUniv	Doctor of the University
EDU	Educational Development Unit
GCE	General Certificate of Education
HNC	Higher National Certificate
HND	Higher National Diploma
HMI	His/Her Majesty's Inspector
ICI	Imperial Chemical Industries Limited
IEE	Institution of Electrical Engineers
ILC	Industrial Liaison Centre
ILO	Industrial Liaison Officer
LCAC	Low-Cost Automation Centre
LGRU	Local Government Research Unit
MACDATA	Materials and Components Development and Testing Association
MAPS	Management and Planning Services

MBA	Master of Business Administration
MEDC	Microelectronics Educational Development Centre
MEP	Members of the European Parliament
MIB	Microelectronics in Business
MIQAL	Microelectronics Quality Assurance Laboratory
MIT	Massachusetts Institute of Technology
MP	Member of Parliament
MSC	Manpower Services Commission
NCTA	National Council for Technological Awards
NEBSS	National Examination Board for Supervisory Studies
NEL	National Engineering Laboratory
ODA	Overseas Development Agency
ONC	Ordinary National Certificate
PACE	Programme for Advanced Continuing Education
PhD	Doctor of Philosophy
RIBA	Royal Institute of British Architects
RICS	Royal Institution of Chartered Surveyors
SANCAD	Scottish Association for National Certificates and Diplomas
SCOT	Scottish College of Textiles
SED	Scottish Education Department
SEEG	Strathclyde Environmental Education Group
SLC	School Leaving Certificate
SRC	Student Representative Council
SSNDT	Scottish School of Non-Destructive Testing
STECC	Scottish Technical Education Consultative Council
TBC	Technology and Business Centre
TEMPUS	Trans-European Mobility Programme for University Studies
VDU	Visual Display Unit

A portrait of Peter Brough by an unknown artist from the
collection of Paisley Museum and Art Gallery.
Reproduced by kind permission of Renfrewshire Council.

Chapter 1
Beginnings

Peter Brough

The story of the University of Paisley begins with a young draper named Peter Brough, only nineteen years of age when he arrived in Paisley. Brough, originally from Scone in Perthshire, had been sent by his Glasgow employer in the early years of the nineteenth century to manage his shop in Paisley. By his 20th birthday Brough had bought the shop, and ten years later he owned six shops, three of them in Paisley.

Peter Brough was shrewd, ambitious and innovative – in 1824 one of his shops became the first in Paisley to have gas lighting – and he was also keenly interested in stocks and shares. By 1839, through hard work and shrewd investment, he was a wealthy man, becoming a member of Paisley Town Council, a Justice of the Peace, a Director of Paisley Water Company, President of the Drapers' Association and Chairman of Paisley Security Savings Bank .

James B. Sturrock, a contemporary and the author of *Peter Brough – A Paisley Philanthropist*,[†] describes Brough as having 'bright, sparkling eyes.' He usually wore a 'navy blue frock coat, black vest and trousers, and was noted for the extreme height of his shirt-collar, which covered the full half of his cheek and was as stiffly starched as Beau Brummell's.'

The Weavers

Peter Brough and Paisley were well suited, for in the nineteenth century the town, like the man, was ambitious and forward-looking. For generations, weaving had been one of its major industries, and round about the time when the local people were marvelling at the sight of the first gas jets burning in young Brough's shop, local weavers were producing the famous Paisley Pattern shawls that made Paisley's name known world-wide.

The Abbey

The town had grown around the Abbey, built in the twelfth century by Walter Fitzalan, High Steward to David I of Scotland, and dedicated to St Mirin, patron saint of Paisley, and St James, patron saint of the Fitzalan family. A descendant of Walter married Marjory, daughter of Robert the

† Sources specifically mentioned in the text are listed in the references and
  bibliography sections at the end of the book.

Bruce, the warrior-king, and their son became the first of the Stewart kings. The House of Stewart (derived from the title of Steward) ruled Scotland, and eventually England, for more than 300 years.

The Abbey enjoyed royal patronage, and during the centuries, a large number of churches throughout the south-west of Scotland were endowed to it. As a result, the Abbey's influence stretched over Renfrewshire, Dunbartonshire, and deep into Ayrshire. At the instigation of Abbot George Schaw, King James IV granted a Royal Charter to Paisley in 1488, making the town a Burgh of Barony and giving it the power to run its own affairs.

The Abbey's days of glory ended in 1560 with the Reformation, which replaced Catholicism with Protestantism as Scotland's main religion. The Abbey became a Protestant church, then fell into disrepair in the eighteenth century. The great boundary wall around its gardens and orchard crumbled and the Paisley people built their new town on former Abbey land, naming the streets – Lawn Street, Silk Street, Gauze Street, Cotton Street – after the materials woven in the town and the surrounding area.

It wasn't until the end of the nineteenth century that work began on repairing and restoring the Abbey. The great drain, itself a magnificent piece of architecture, yielded various items, including a piece of slate with polyphonic music scratched on it, believed to be the oldest artefact of its kind found in Scotland so far.

Paisley Benefactors

Paisley has had many benefactors in its time, the best-known during the nineteenth and early twentieth centuries being the Clarks and the Coats, two powerful thread-making families The development of the thread industry is said to have been helped by information brought to Paisley from Holland in the early eighteenth century by Christian Shaw, a young widow who, in childhood, had been the central player in the district's most famous witch-hunt.

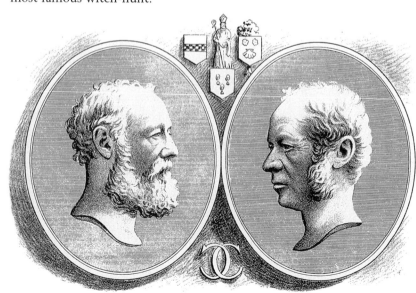

Sir Peter and Thomas Coats depicted in *The Bailie* in 1881. It was the next generation of the Coats family who supported the College. Sir Thomas Glen-Coats, Major A Harold Glen-Coats, P Herbert Coats and James Coats, Junior were all members of the Board of Governors.

The Clark and Coats families both emerged from humble beginnings to become world-famous, and both dynasties left their mark on the town in the form of mills, mansions, churches, parks, gardens and schools. The George A Clark Town Hall, adjacent to the Abbey, was built mainly with money from the Clark family, while the Coats built, among other things, the library and museum, the Observatory, and Coats Memorial Baptist Church.

Education

In the nineteenth century Paisley, like other towns of its size, had a motley collection of parish and privately endowed schools. Principal among them were the Grammar School, founded by Charter in 1576, the English or Writing School and Paisley Commercial School (both derived from the Grammar), Hutcheson's Charity School (1804), the John Neilson Institution (1852) and Camphill School (1888). The Neilson and Hutcheson's schools were the result of private endowments. Paisley Grammar is the only one of these original schools still in existence.

The Grammar, Commercial, English and Hutcheson's schools all stood near to each other, almost forming a very early campus, in the town's Oakshaw district, a terrace above and parallel to the High Street. A number of churches were also built at Oakshawhill, and several of the wealthier townspeople, including draper Peter Brough, built their fine homes there.

In 1872 a new Education Act made education compulsory for children between the ages of 5 and 13, and brought all schools under the control of School Boards. Paisley's Education Board then built four new state schools to the east, west, north and south of the town.

Further Education

Lectures were held in the Philosophical Institution, founded in 1808. Equipped with books and scientific apparatus, it was frequented by amateur scientists, scholars and local industrialists, one of whom was Thomas Coats,

The Government School of Design, Gilmour Street, Paisley. Opened on the 4th December, 1848. Now demolished.

a keen amateur astronomer. He built the Coats Observatory in 1882 and presented it to the Institution, together with an endowment of two thousand pounds.

The Artisans' Institute (1847) ran evening classes and held Society of Arts examinations. In the 1880s Paisley Provident Co-operative Society set up a library and reading room, and, in the 1890s, started evening classes in dressmaking and cookery.

By the end of the nineteenth century evening classes were being held in the Grammar School, Oakshaw School and Camphill School.

School of Design

An attempt to form a School of Arts in the town failed in 1836, but a second attempt in 1846, this time for a School of Design, met with more success; a committee was elected and applied to the President and Council of the Government School of Design in London, pointing out that the majority of Paisley's population was employed in the manufacture of shawls and fabrics, machine-making and iron-founding, all involving design.

The application met with success, and a site in Gilmour Street was bought for £500. The building and its furnishings cost £2,500 and public subscriptions to raise the money reached £1,800, which meant that the school opened in December 1848 with a debt of £1,200.

William Stewart

A self-portrait of William Stewart from the collection of Paisley Museum and Art Gallery.

A talented and able young man, William Stewart was only 25 years of age when he took over his duties as headmaster of the new Government School of Design. He had trained in Edinburgh School of Art and at the Royal Academy in London, and had taught in Norwich before returning to Scotland. During his 33 years in Paisley he helped to found Paisley Art Institute, and was its first president.

As had happened with other Government Schools of Design, not all the local manufacturers were happy about the school's remit. Quentin Bell says in his book, *The Schools of Design*, that some manufacturers and workmen saw the schools as a criticism of the quality of their own work, or an opportunity for rival textile companies to improve their position at public expense. Shawl manufacturer Robert Kerr resigned from the committee in protest because he foresaw the school as giving more tuition in sculpture and fine arts than in dealing with local issues, and other manufacturers were unhappy with the prospect of advanced students in their employment disclosing details of their work in the classroom.

James Elder Christie

The school's most famous student was James Elder Christie (1847-1914) who studied under William Stewart and later worked in the town as a photographer. Brought to Paisley as a child by his mother and stepfather, Christie was blessed with a lively imagination, and created a series of political

A sketch of James Elder Christie from *The Bailie*. 1896.

cartoons published in *The Hoolet*, a local publication.

Realising that art meant more to him than photography, Christie moved to London where he was a gold medallist at the Royal Academy. After living for a time in Paris he settled in Glasgow, where he became President of the Glasgow Art Club.

An article in the *Scots Pictorial* of January 1900 marking his appointment describes Christie as 'big, burly and genial.' Over six feet tall, broad-shouldered and bearded, he was a great admirer of Rabbie Burns. His passionate rendering of the poet's *Tam o' Shanter* was much in demand at gatherings, and one of his most famous paintings features Tam drinking with his cronies.

From Paisley's point of view, the best known of Christie's works is *Paisley Cross, 1868*, which features a large number of prominent townspeople of the time. Sir Peter Coats, who presented the Museum and Art Gallery to the townspeople, bought Christie's painting, which hangs today in the Art Gallery, almost opposite the University.

In 1852 Britain's Schools of Design were renamed Schools of Art, then Schools of Art and Science, the art section mainly covering ornamental art as industrial design, for use in the manufacture of textiles and carpets.

Technical Education

Until 1901 scientific and technical education in Britain was controlled by the London-based Department of Science and Art, which had sole responsibility for inspecting schools and awarding grants to the science departments of well established schools like Paisley Grammar and to institutions like the Schools of Design.

In 1864, however, the Department decided to withdraw its grant system and replace it with payments on teaching results. This came as a blow to Paisley's School of Design, as it meant that from then on the salaries of William Stewart and his teaching staff would have to come from students' fees. As time passed, the school began to diversify, possibly in an attempt to attract students. Mechanical and architectural classes had been introduced in 1851/52, and in 1878 classes in chemistry and in magnetism and electricity began. By 1882, with 274 students studying art and science in the evenings, and some art classes held during the day for ladies, science subjects were overtaking art subjects.

In 1881 a serious drop in enrolments forced William Stewart's resignation as there was not sufficient revenue from fees to pay his salary. He retired to Greenock, and died in 1906 at the age of 83. An obituary in the *Paisley and Renfrewshire Gazette* notes that, as headmaster of the Design School, Mr Stewart taught most of the town's pattern-drawers and designers, and goes on to say that despite his 'somewhat distant manner', his students were ultimately drawn to him by his enthusiastic interest in their work.

The European Threat

The 1878 International Exhibition in Paris clearly spelled out to British industrialists and educationalists that European countries, particularly Germany, were leading the field in terms of science and technology. Already a number of workers from other countries, including clerical workers, were employed throughout Britain because they possessed skills that their contemporaries simply could not match.

In 1880 a candidate at a Paisley School Board election meeting spoke of his concern over what he called 'the German plague' of clerks working in the town, and a few years later the Samuelson Report on technical instruction (1884) urged that industrial workers in Britain should be well instructed in theory as well as in practical work. Most of the schools under the jurisdiction of the new School Boards covered elementary, or primary, education, but there was a recognised need for higher grade schools with wider curriculums.

In 1884 Aberdeen's Mechanics Institution merged with Robert Gordon's College to form a larger technical institution, and in the following year the endowments of the Watt Institution and Heriot's Hospital in Edinburgh were amalgamated to create the Heriot Watt College. In 1886, in the year that the last harness shawl was being woven on a Paisley loom, several Glasgow institutions merged to become the Glasgow and West of Scotland Technical College, and in 1887, while Peter Coats was building his half-time school at Ferguslie to provide ongoing education for his younger mill employees, the various classes of the Dundee Mechanics Institute were merged into a new Dundee Technical Institute.

The call for certain technical skills to be taught in educational institutions as well as in factories did not meet with approval from all industrialists. Many clung to tradition, which decreed that artisans should learn their trade in the work-place while education, in the form of the three Rs, should be provided by schools.

Before 1878 the Scotch Education Department (a title that must surely set many a Scottish tooth on edge) was based in London and worked in conjunction with a Board in Edinburgh. From 1878 until 1885 it was controlled by the London-based Committee of the Privy Council on Education, and in 1885 Scotland's first Secretary (the title was changed to Secretary of State for Scotland in 1926) was appointed and given powers as vice-president of the Scotch Education Department (SED). The Secretary's appointment marked a step forward for Scottish education.

When Henry Craik, the first SED Secretary, introduced the School Leaving Certificate (SLC) in 1888, School Boards began to develop higher-grade schools where children could be taught to SLC level. In Paisley, the Grammar, the Neilson and Camphill were higher-grade schools.

The Brough Bequests

Peter Brough, the draper who had made his fortune, and his mark, in Paisley, died in July 1883. He left a considerable number of bequests to Paisley's benefit, among them the direction that his house was to become a home for nurses, and that an annual sum of £300 be used for the establishment and maintenance of a science lectureship within the Burgh of Paisley. He left the final decision on subjects to be taught to his trustees, though he himself recommended that they should include physiology. The balance of his wealth was to be used by his trustees as they saw fit.

The Brough Trustees, a group of highly-regarded Paisley businessmen, made a momentous decision. They agreed to combine the £300 for the science lectureship with the balance of the estate, and use the money to set up a much-needed Technical School for Paisley.

Peter Brough's memorial stone stands in Woodside Cemetery, and reads, 'Erected in Memory of Peter Brough Esquire, of Oakshawhead House, Paisley. Born 25th September 1797, Died 18th July 1883.' A 1902 article in the *Paisley and Renfrewshire Gazette* refers to the stone as being 'worthy of notice,' and recalls Brough as an old man, 'dressed in unfashionable and sometimes worn clothing, . . . perhaps as good a specimen of the genus miser as ever existed outside the pages of fiction. . . .' The article, however, says that 'nothing in his life became him half so well as the disposal of his wealth,' and admits that '. . . the streams of benefaction (from his large fortune) run as refreshingly through Paisley today as does the water system. . . .'

Peter Brough is not as well remembered as other local benefactors, partly because he left no children and grandchildren to carry his name down through the ages, partly because his talent lay not in manufacturing but in selling goods that others had made, and partly because in life he was a quiet, withdrawn man. But the terms of his will and the far-sightedness of his Trustees were to affect Paisley as just as much as the philanthropy of the Clarks and the Coats.

The New Technical School

In 1884 the Brough Trustees made an offer to the School of Design's hard-pressed Board of Directors. They would provide substantial aid for the School in return for an agreement that the Board of Governors would sell their Gilmour Street premises and combine with the Trustees to acquire a new site, preferably in the High Street, for an institution of art, science and, so far as possible, technical instruction, adequate to the wants of the community. They offered £1,500 towards the cost of such a building, and a possible £200 per year to assist in its maintenance.

Although it ultimately turned out to be a bad move as far as the School of Design was concerned, its Board agreed in principle, and in May 1885, the year the new Municipal County Buildings were built in St James' Street and the first tram rails were laid in Paisley, the Design School building in Gilmour Street was sold to the Town Council for £4,000 on the understanding that the School could rent the building back for £60 per annum for as long as it was required. The search for premises for a new Paisley Technical and Art School was on.

Technical Schools Act

In 1886 the Technical Schools (Scotland) Act backed the Samuelson Report by emphasising the need to teach theory as well as practical work. Opening Camphill School on April 14, 1888, Sir John Neilson Cuthbertson, Chairman of the Glasgow School Board, spoke of the way in which the new school could, through evening classes, give apprentices and others a wider knowledge of the trades in which they worked.

In October 1892 Sheriff Hugh Cowan, at that time Chairman of the Brough Trust, returned from a visit to North American technical institutions and reported to his fellow trustees that at MIT (Massachusetts Institute of Technology) and in Toronto and, indeed, at the Yorkshire College in Leeds, machinery and building materials were being tested for 'outside bodies.' He suggested that similar work could be carried out by Paisley's proposed new technical school in the interests of both the public and the school. Such a scheme, he said, would provide a source of revenue while linking the school to the life and work of the community.

Sadly, his fellow trustees were not inclined to take up his idea, and many decades were to pass before it was finally, and very successfully, put into practice.

Early in 1890 the search for suitable premises for the new technical school ended, when J & P Coats, one of the town's leading textile manufacturers, made a gift to the Brough Trustees of a disused dye-works in George Street, close to the junction with Storie Street. With the site and building came a further generous gift of £3,000 towards the erection of the new school building.

This sign on the gable of the Lady Lane residences is the only visible evidence of the St. Mirren Burn which runs underground through the Paisley Campus. In the nineteenth Century its waters served the dyeworks and reservoir which were located to the west of 'G' Block, approximately where 'D' Block, the Elles Building and TBC now stand. When the dyeworks closed Coats donated the land to the Brough Trustees and it was used as the site of the Technical School.

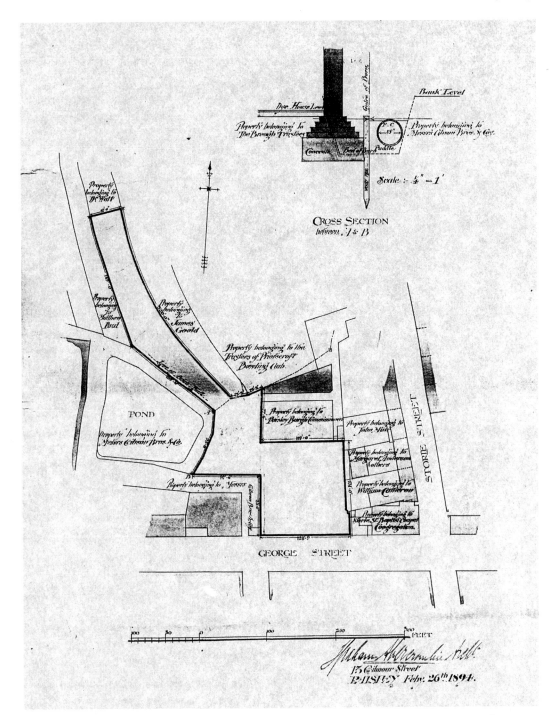

A plan attached to the title deeds of the property given by Coats to the Brough Trustees. It was drawn in 1894 by TG Abercrombie and shows the adjoining landowners and a cross-section of the culverted St. Mirren Burn.

Archibald Barr

By then, the trustees had accumulated £7,000 and were hopeful of supplementing it with the residual resources from the School of Design, if agreement could be reached with its Board of Directors. They commissioned a specification from local architect T. Graham Abercrombie and sought advice from Professor Archibald Barr, born in Paisley and educated at the John Neilson Institution and Glasgow University.

Barr, who had served his engineering apprenticeship in Paisley, had been Professor of Civil and Mechanical Engineering in the Yorkshire College of Science, now Leeds University, for five years before taking up a post as lecturer in the Civil and Mechanical Engineering Department at Glasgow University in 1889. At Leeds he had met Professor William Stroud, a physicist; in 1909 the two men were to set up the well-known firm of Barr and Stroud.

Archibald Barr considered the George Street site to be ideal for the proposed school, and recommended the purchase of the Paisley Baths site and the Baptist Church site on the corner of Storie Street and George Street for further expansion, should they ever become available. He advocated a cautious building programme, with permanent premises for the School of Art already in existence, and temporary accommodation for science-based courses until such time as they proved to be popular.

The Board of Governors

At the first meeting of the new Board of Governors in January 1895 five Board members were elected by the Brough Trust, two by the School of Design, one each from Paisley Town Council and the Philosophical Institution, and two elected by J & P Coats, in recognition of their financial donation and gift of the site.

The rest of the Board consisted of three ex-officio members, one of them being Provost Archibald MacKenzie who was himself a Paisley benefactor, having built and equipped the Royal Victoria Eye Infirmary and gifted it to the town. Five further members, known as the Governors' nominees, were elected, and Sheriff Cowan, Chairman of Paisley Education Trust, became Chairman of the Board, while James Gardner, Secretary of the Brough Trustees and a partner in the highly-regarded Paisley legal firm of J & A Gardner, was appointed Secretary and Treasurer. The strong link between the Technical School/College and the Gardner firm was to last until the early 1960s.

The Board of Governors represented a good mix of local industry. There were starch manufacturers, feuars, church representatives, bankers, shawl manufacturers, solicitors, hatters, jam manufacturers, thread manufacturers, accountants, engineers and foundry-men, dyers, and packing manufacturers.

Archibald Barr's suggestion of temporary accommodation was set aside, and by the middle of the year nine architects from Paisley and Glasgow had been invited to take part in an open competition to design the new school building. The Board had decided on three departmental headings for the new school – Art (drawing and shading, painting from nature,

THE GLASGOW INSTITUTE OF THE FINE ARTS.

TWO DESIGNS IN COMPETITION FOR PAISLEY TECHNICAL SCHOOL.

(No. 298). DESIGN BY MESSRS. CAMPBELL DOUGLAS & MORRISON.

(No. 322). DESIGN BY MESSRS. JOHN HONEYMAN & KEPPIE.

Two unsuccessful designs for the Paisley Technical School as they appeared in *Building Industry*, March 16th 1897. One of Honeyman and Keppie's designs came second.

drawing and painting from life, freehand, perspective and geometrical model drawing, and designing for architects and designers), Chemistry and Physics, and a Science Department covering machine construction, magnetism and electricity, building construction and drawing, carpentry and joinery, brick and mason work, naval architecture, mechanical engineering, steam and steam engines, and applied and theoretical mechanics. Additional subjects and practical training for craft-based subjects were listed as possible future developments.

Dr Rowand Anderson (later to become Sir Rowand Anderson) of Edinburgh was invited to judge the architectural competition. Dr Anderson had designed the National Portrait Gallery and the National Museum of Antiquities as well as Glasgow's Central Hotel and the Pearce Institute in Govan.

Thomas Abercrombie

First place in the competition went to Paisley architect Thomas Graham Abercrombie, who had drawn up the original specifications for the Governors. The son of a local banker, he was born in 1852 and apprenticed at the age of sixteen to Glasgow architect John Hutchison, who had an eye for a good apprentice – some six years later he was to take on a lad by the name of Charles Rennie Mackintosh.

After a spell in America, Abercrombie returned to Paisley in 1886 to set up his own firm. In 1888 he and his partner, Robert S. Symington, won a competition to design Greenlaw Church, and in 1894 they designed Paisley's Royal Alexandra Infirmary, together with its nurses' home and dispensary. In 1896 the firm designed the present Grammar School building in Glasgow Road and in 1897, the Territorial Army Drill Hall.

Other local examples of Abercrombie's architectural work include Wallneuk Church (1913), Hunterhill House (1902), the YMCA buildings in New Street (1907) and the Bird in the Hand Hotel in nearby Johnstone, designed in 1910.

T G Abercrombie as photographed in 1910.

TG, as his friends knew him, was a keen rugby player and a member of the local volunteer force, rising to the rank of Captain of the 2nd Renfrewshire Rifle Volunteers. Co-founder of the first Boys' Brigade company in the town, Abercrombie died in 1926.

Fourth place in the competition, together with an honourable mention, went to another Paisley-born architect, W.D. McLennan, who had by then moved to Ireland. Mr McLennan, a contemporary of Charles Rennie Mackintosh, designed St Matthew's Church and the Bull Inn in New Street, then known as the Black Bull Inn, hard by Abercrombie's YMCA Building. He received a prize of 15 guineas for his Technical School entry.

The cost of the proposed new school, incorporating a lecture hall with accommodation for 300 students,

T G Abercrombie's design for the Technical school from *Building Industry*. April 18th 1896. Note the proposed decorative spire.

was estimated at £18,600. In February 1897 the Board of Governors applied to the Department of Science and Art for a building grant, only to be rejected. All the funds had already been allocated for 1897/8 and 1898/9, and only reduced grants would be available for the following three years before the buildings grants were discontinued altogether. Despite this setback work went ahead.

Foundations

On November 30th 1897, a wet and windy day, Princess Louise, Marchioness of Lorne and 6th child of Queen Victoria, travelled to Paisley with her husband, the Marquis of Lorne and future Duke of Argyll, to carry out two duties – the formal opening of the Brough Home for Nurses in the morning and then, after lunch in the George A. Clark Town Hall, laying the new Technical School's foundation stone.

The Princess wore a black silk accordion-pleated skirt, a black velvet Russian blouse trimmed with sable and set off by a creamy lace jabot, and a black velvet hat decorated with ostrich feathers, wings and petunia roses. The Lady's Pictorial described her as 'looking young and graceful'; a member of the public, as reported in the *Paisley and Renfrewshire Gazette*, thought that she looked, 'awfu' plain, but awfu' nice.'

A glass jar containing all the coins of the realm, details of the Governors and the contractors, copies of the invitations and platform cards, a *Guide to Paisley*, a copy of the *Deed of Constitution*, and copies of the *Paisley and Renfrewshire Gazette, Glasgow Herald, North British Daily Mail, Scotsman, Daily Record, Glasgow Evening Citizen, Glasgow Evening Times, Glasgow Evening News* and *Paisley Daily Express*, was placed within a cavity in the foundation stone. Sadly, the exact site of the stone is unknown; the general

PRINCESS LOUISE'S VISIT TO PAISLEY.

SKETCHES BY OUR SPECIAL ARTIST.

At the Brough Home the Princess Louise is presented with a bouquet.

The Members of Lorne replying for the Princess.

At the Technical School The Princess laying the memorial stone.

ROYAL VISIT TO PAISLEY.

Princess Louise and Lord Lorne.

The Provost

Princess Louise visit to Paisley as depicted in *The Evening Times* for Wednesday December 1st 1897.

consensus is that during one of the school/college/university's expansion programmes somebody unwittingly built on top of it. Suffice it to say that the foundation stone is on the original George Street site.

In the year the stone was laid, the Department of Science and Art was absorbed into the Department of Education. In that same year an article in the *Education News* warned that Britain must outstrip Germany in the provision of means of training its citizens for 'the battle of commerce. Technical schools, adapted for every variety of industry, must be spread like a network over the land . . . the aim of education must be directly to qualify the pupils for their work in life.'

F. Grant Ogilvie

Paisley was doing its best. In 1898 the Board of Governors consulted F. Grant Ogilvie, Principal of Heriot Watt College in Edinburgh, as to what subjects should be taught in the new school. After visiting the town Mr Ogilvie advised that the Grammar School and the John Neilson Institution should continue to provide scientific and technical instruction for their more advanced day scholars while the Technical School concentrated on evening classes in science and art, as well as any technical and commercial subjects of importance to local industry.

He felt, however, that the advanced course evening classes then run by the School Board at Camphill School should be transferred to the Technical School once it opened because of the advantages of holding such classes in one well-equipped and centralised institution.

To the subjects already proposed by the Board, he added Commercial Practice and Book-keeping, French and Shorthand. He also advocated the introduction, in the future, of higher work, especially in the established classes to be inherited from the School of Design, and future classes in Sound, Heat and Light, Natural Science, English Composition and Commercial Correspondence and German, as well as Handicraft classes for apprentices.

He estimated the total cost of staffing and overheads to be £1,200, the money to come from grants of £500 from the Brough Trust, £150 from the Town Council, £200 from class fees and £350 from Government grants.

In January 1899 the Board formally adopted Mr Ogilvie's recommendations and went on to advertise the post of Principal.

The original Technical School Building, No 28-40 George Street as photographed in the early 1960s. It is now known as the Gardner Building or 'G' Block.

Chapter 2
Principal Angus McLean
(1899 -1929)

Paisley Technical School Principalship
The Governors of the Paisley Technical School invite applications from gentlemen qualified in Science or Technical Work for the Post of Principal. The successful Candidate shall devote his whole time to the duties of the Office, and shall himself teach certain subjects, so as to occupy his time on Five Evenings per Week. Salary, £300 per annum. The School will be opened about the month of September, and the successful Candidate must then be prepared to enter on duty. Further particulars may be obtained from the Subscriber, with whom Applications and 12 Copies of Testimonials must be lodged on or before 13th February. The Governors strongly object to canvassing of every description.

James Gardner, Solicitor,
Secretary to the Governors.
Friday, 20th January 1899

Out of 53 applicants, the Governors appointed Angus McLean BSc (Hons.) as the first Principal of Paisley Technical School.

The new Principal, 35 years of age at the time of his appointment in March 1899, was a native of Tarbert, Loch Fyne and a graduate of Glasgow University, where he was a distinguished student, winning bursaries, prizes and exhibitions. After graduating with a BSc (Hons.) in Mathematics and Natural Philosophy he worked as an assistant in Lord Kelvin's laboratories before becoming assistant to the Professor of Natural Philosophy in Glasgow Technical College, then a lecturer and demonstrator in Experimental Physics.

Angus McLean had no wish to staff his school entirely with School of Design teachers. In a report to the Governors shortly after his appointment, he made it clear that he intended to run the new Technical School in his own way. 'The selection of staff is a matter to which careful, and early, attention must be given,' he wrote. 'The success of the school will largely depend on the efficiency and energy of the teachers. I have interviewed almost all the teachers in the

Principal Angus
McLean

late School of Design. I think some of these might be asked to fill positions on our staff.

'As janitor, a man with a practical knowledge of the working of machinery will be requisite, and I think it would be an additional qualification if he could repair apparatus and do work of a similar kind should occasion require.

'I . . . express my firm conviction that the success of the school will in no small degree depend upon our giving the students to understand from the first that we can supply advanced as well as elementary education in all the branches of study, thereby making them feel that it is unnecessary for them to go further afield when what they require is provided for them at home.'

Nor was he eager to take on the School of Design's craft classes. In his view there was a need to secure support from local employers before craft and 'technological' classes such as plumbing, carpentry and joinery, and electric light wiring could be undertaken, since they were not grant-earning. The Governors duly sent out a circular to local companies, pointing out that they must play their part in the establishment of such classes. The response, however, was poor, and the classes were postponed for the time being.

McLean's reference to the importance of local students being given the further education they required close to home shows that he was aware of the close proximity of the City of Glasgow, with its famous old university and its many colleges. Paisley had always lived in its shadow and, watching Glasgow swallow up whole villages and communities as it expanded, the Paisley folk had grown all the more determined not to be drawn into its maw. In 1500 Paisley Abbey had to appeal to the Pope for justice when the Archbishop of Glasgow started demanding rents from its endowed churches. When electric tramway routes were proposed between Glasgow and Paisley in 1898, the Paisley people at first opposed the plan, suspicious of what they saw as another attempt at a Glasgow takeover.

Bright students from the Paisley schools had tended to go on to Glasgow University for their further education; clearly McLean harboured an ambition to provide Paisley students with a good higher education in their own town.

McLean himself remained a keen student; not long after his appointment as Principal he entered a London University examination and gained a first-class honours degree in Experimental Physics, achieving the highest marks given to any candidate in that subject. In 1912 he published a text book on practical physics for technical colleges.

Insisting that the new Art Master must be directly answerable to him and not to the Governors, McLean travelled to London to interview applicants personally before appointing James Ness to the position. Ness, a painter and sculptor, exhibited his work frequently at the Royal Glasgow Institute of Fine Arts, including, in 1907, a portrait of Angus McLean himself.

The First Term

On October 2nd 1899, Paisley Technical School opened its doors to students, its first prospectus stating firmly that the intention was, 'To provide advanced instruction in the various branches of Science, Art and Technology and to be the means, for the inhabitants of Paisley and the surrounding district, of obtaining a sound education in Science and Art and such Technological subjects as have a special relation to the industries of the neighbourhood.'

Seven hundred and sixteen students attended in the school's first month, covering 1,059 class enrolments. The Town Council gave notification of its intention to award a grant of £800 for the current year, and the County Council's Secondary Education Department awarded a grant of £20 plus fifteen shillings (75p) capitation per student, conditional on the introduction of a class on agriculture.

Most of the classes were held in the evenings, with art the only subject taught during the day until 1912. The only full-time members of staff in those early years were Angus McLean, James Ness, and the janitor. The ten part-time staff members included teachers from the Glasgow and West of Scotland Technical College, Glasgow Athenaeum, local secondary schools and local industry. Some were from the staff of Glasgow University. Angus McLean was well acquainted with Sir Donald MacAlister, a lecturer at the University and Principal from 1907-1929, since their fathers had worked on the same estate in Tarbert.

Textile manufacturing was important in Paisley at the beginning of the twentieth century, and a course in textile engineering had been set up in the technical school in response to a direct approach from J. & P. Coats (now merged with Clark's thread company). Engineering, shipbuilding, and the manufacture of foodstuffs and chemicals had established themselves as local industries during the final decades of the nineteenth century, and the Arrol Johnson company began manufacturing motor vehicles at their Underwood Works not long after 1900.

During the opening years of the century, until the outbreak of war there was general expansion in the West of Scotland, particularly in heavy industry. It had always been intended that the new Technical School would develop its scientific and engineering departments in line with these growth industries.

School of Design

Now that the Technical School was in operation there was no longer any need for the School of Design. From that first approach by the Brough Trustees in 1883 it had been doomed. An attempt by its directors to have equal standing with the Brough Trustees on the new Technical School Board had been rejected, and from the time the new Board of Governors was formally constituted they had sought assurance from the Town Council that when the School of Design closed, its grants would be transferred to the Technical School.

On April 2nd 1900 the inevitable happened – the School of Design was formally dissolved.

Official Opening

In November 1900 the Duke of Argyll, who as the Marquis of Lorne had watched his Royal wife lay the Technical School's foundation stone three years earlier, officially opened the Technical School.

Angus McLean maintained his tight grip of the reins. He was responsible for the recruiting and registering of students, appointing staff, supervising the preparation of the syllabus, preparing official returns (which included calculating eligibility for financial grants), and the care and maintenance of the building.

He also taught Mathematics, Dynamics and Experimental Physics, and was in the building until 10 p.m. on most evenings during the week. The Governors must have been confident that their first Principal was indeed 'occupying his time,' as laid down in their original advertisement.

An enthusiastic description of the new building can be found in a chapter on Angus McLean in *Captains of Industry*, by William S. Murphy (1901):- 'Externally the building has a fine appearance, with a front of three storeys, not too pretentious, but solidly ornamented. The ground floor is occupied by the office, board-room, the Principal's private room, and the various branches of the Art Department. Round the walls of the designing room are hung splendid specimens of textile designs lent from the South Kensington Art Museum. In the modelling-room are casts, frescoes, panels and other requisites of the modeller's art. The large art room, 73 ft. long,

Chemical Laboratory from the 1902/3 *Technical School Calendar*.

can be divided into two apartments if required, one section being regularly
used as a life-room. Not only are the rooms of this school spacious, finely
lighted by electric lamps specially designed, lined throughout by varnished
wood and equipped with suitable desks and benches, but the Art
Department has models of the highest class, the science teachers have at
hand chemicals, instruments of all kinds for experiment, demonstration
and illustration; the naval instructor possesses a water tank and models to
illustrate his lectures; . . . every lecturer has ample means of enforcing his
arguments and fixing his teachings in the minds of his pupils.'

Then comes a barb aimed at local industry. 'If criticism of so admirable
an institution may be permitted we should say that the Technological
Department is very small compared with Science and Art. . . . In such an
industrial centre a deficiency of that kind cannot long be deemed excusable.
It is for the industrial leaders of Paisley to take the matter up. . . . With so
many facilities for expansion, and an enthusiastic Principal at its head, this
Technical School bids fair to be the *alma mater* of industry in Paisley and
district. In addition to the nobler incentives and ample aids to study, the
Brough Trustees offer scholarships varying in value from £3 to £5 to students
who, by faithful attendance and proficiency in examination, prove their
merit.'

Thomas S. Tait

Arguably the most famous student to attend Paisley's Technical School
was architect Thomas S. Tait, born in Paisley in 1882 and educated in the
John Neilson Institution. In the school's 1899/1900 list of prize-winners
he appears twice as a student in the Science Department, sharing second

Thomas S Tait in the 1930s. Photograph by kind permission of the *Glasgow Herald* and *The Evening Times*.

place in the elementary stage scholarship on Practical Plane and Solid Geometry and taking first place in the advanced stage scholarship in Building Construction.

While studying in Paisley he won national competition prizes in architectural design and sculpture: in 1901 he was the sole Scottish winner of the King's Prize in Ornamental Design, and during the 1902/3 session he was a committee member of Paisley Technical School Art Club, an association for present and former students. In 1902 the School Calendar notes his appointment to John Burnet & Son, Glasgow architects, and during the 1904/5 session he appears in the Calendar as a lecturer and instructor in architecture and architectural design.

Tait completed his education at Glasgow School of Art and the Royal Academy School in London, then became personal assistant to London-based architect Sir John Burnet. In time he became Sir John's chief assistant, then a full partner of Sir John Burnet, Tait and Lorne in 1920. The firm designed a number of war memorials for the Imperial War Graves Commission as well as many fine London buildings, including the Lloyds Bank headquarters, Adelaide House, and the Colonial Office.

Elementary Art Room 1902 from the *Technical School Calendar*.

In 1932 Thomas Tait designed Paisley's Infectious Diseases Hospital at Hawkhead and in the following year he won a competition to design the St Andrew's House buildings in Edinburgh. He was also involved in the architectural designs of London Bridge and the pylons of Sydney Harbour Bridge.

In 1938 he was appointed the controlling architect for the Glasgow Empire Exhibition (one of the major subscribers to the Exhibition was J & P Coats, of Paisley), planning the site overall and designing many of the pavilions. He also designed the exhibition's magnificent centre-piece, a tower which soared 300 feet above Bellahouston Park and afforded a superb view of the exhibition and the surrounding area to those who travelled in its lifts to the top. The tower was officially known as the Tower of Empire, but the Scots themselves gave it the name by which it is still known – Tait's Tower.

'Nothing in the exhibition,' says the official *Exhibition Guide*, 'has so caught the public imagination as the Tower.' Delicate yet strong, pleasing to the eye, it was illuminated after dark throughout the exhibition, piercing the night sky and serving as a fitting tribute to Tait's architectural brilliance.

Thomas Tait died in 1954, aged 72 years.

Pat Dollan, Glasgow Council's Treasurer at the time of the exhibition, and later Sir Patrick Dollan, the city's Lord Provost, wanted the Tower and some other structures to remain after the exhibition ended; to this day many regret that he did not get his way. In 1995 Councillor Pat Lally, then Glasgow's Council Leader, suggested that Tait's Tower should be rebuilt. 'It would be a tremendous tourist attraction,' he said, '. . . just as the Eiffel Tower is synonymous with Paris . . . Tait's Tower would automatically be associated with Glasgow.'

In view of their struggles in the past to remain independent from Glasgow, the Paisley people may not be over enthusiastic about a local man's creation being regarded as a Glasgow triumph!

'Tait's Tower' at the Empire Exhibition held in 1938 in Bellahouston Park, Glasgow. Reproduced by kind permission of Classic Cards (formerly Valentines of Dundee).

The Central Institutions

In 1901 the Secretary of the Scotch Education Department introduced the Code of Regulations for Continuation Classes, aimed at drawing primary, secondary and further education together under the SED's control. Among other things the Code gave the SED the power to grant, at its discretion, special financial aid to any technical school or College giving advanced instruction linked with industry. These favoured institutions were to be known as Central Institutions (CIs) and the first to be so honoured were the Glasgow and West of Scotland Technical College, the Heriot Watt College in Edinburgh and the Dundee Technical Institution and School of Art. In 1903 the Robert Gordon's College and Gray's School of Art (both in Aberdeen), Glasgow Athenaeum Commercial College, Leith Nautical College and the three agricultural colleges all became CIs.

Lord Balfour of Burleigh, then Secretary for Scotland, said that the SED's aim was to make its CIs 'centres of the most advanced instruction possible in the various branches of technical knowledge . . . and for this purpose they should be relieved of the burden of instructing elementary students whose wants could be provided in other institutions.'

Although Paisley Technical School's Governors denied that they wanted CI status, they sought exemption from the limitations placed on continuation classes, pointing out that they had never intended the school to be 'a mere continuation school.'

The SED's response was cool, but the Governors continued to press their claim while at the same time asking the SED for a building grant of £1,500, as they wanted to develop the old dye-works as a technological wing. The SED agreed to grant the money, but the Carnegie Trust, also approached, turned down the appeal.

The plans for the new wing caused dissension among the Governors. In 1902 John Hodgart, a partner in the engineering firm of Fullerton, Hodgart and Barclay, resigned from the Board in protest against the inclusion of a

'On the recommendation of Principal McLean it was agreed to organise classes for . . . the degree of Bachelor of Science of London University' An extract from the Minutes of a meeting of the Board of Governors, 12th June 1903.

> On the recommendation of Principal McLean it was agreed to organise classes for the Matriculation, Intermediate & Final Examinations for the degree of Bachelor of Science of London University. Mr. James Moffat B.Sc. (Lond.), 19 Newton Street, Greenock was appointed to take charge of the Matriculation Science classes at a salary of £40 & Mr Thomas Reid, M.A., to take charge of the Matriculation French classes at a salary of £20. It was left to the Principal to select a suitable teacher for the Matriculation English class at a salary of £20.

Mechanical Engineering laboratory which, he felt, would serve no practical purpose. He wasn't the only industrialist convinced at that time that practical work could only be learned on the factory floor and that technical institutions should confine themselves to theory.

The London University Degree

In 1904 Angus McLean's ambitions for his school led to an important step forward when London University recognised Paisley Technical School as an external centre for some of its science and engineering courses leading to matriculation, intermediate and final examination for its BSc degree.

The link between university and technical school, which was to last for more than 60 years, brought distinction to the new Paisley institution, as well as introducing the need for classes in English and modern languages.

New Title

From 1904 Paisley Technical School called itself Paisley Technical College and School of Art, despite the SED's argument that the title would clash with the Glasgow and West of Scotland Technical College. Until the 1930s the Governors were to be irked by the SED's insistence on retaining the old title of Paisley Technical School in its official correspondence.

As the terms passed, student enrolment numbers grew, and in the 1905/6 session five separate departments were created – Mechanical Engineering, Naval Architecture, Electrical Engineering, Chemistry, and Building Construction. Each had its own Head of Department, but the posts were still part-time, with only the Principal, the Art Master and the janitor employed on a full-time basis.

John Denholm

In 1904 John Denholm, a teacher born in Berwickshire, moved to Paisley with his family, teaching first in Kilmacolm, then in Paisley's Camphill School before being appointed as the College's part-time evening Registrar and Librarian. The part-time appointment, intended to ease the Principal's growing burden of responsibilities, seemed a small matter at the time, but was eventually to bless the College with far-reaching benefits.

Financial problems

Despite its growth, the College was in a vulnerable financial situation. It had been in debt since its inauguration, and unlike the CIs it had no direct funding from central government grants or from local interests. The Governors were exasperated by the SED's suggestion that Paisley's role should lie in providing instruction suitable for the town's craftsmen and preparing a few selected students for more advanced instruction at a Central Institution in Glasgow.

In turn, the SED, as Dr David Graham reports in his thesis, *The Origins and Development of Paisley College of Technology (1895-1980)* were irritated by the way the College ignored the Group Certificate system set up by the

Camphill School which formerly stood on the site of the present Castlehead High School in Paisley.

SED in 1903, and continued to enrol students in single subjects.

However, they did support the College in one area. In 1901 the SED's Assistant Secretary and HMI (His Majesty's Inspector) had approved the idea of centralisation within Paisley of science and technical evening classes at the College; the local School Board, however, possibly feeling that their schools were under threat from the College just as the College was under threat from Glasgow, deferred action on the matter.

In 1905, following indifferent examination results in science and technical subjects at Camphill School's evening classes, the SED put pressure on the School Board, and it was agreed that the Board's provision in engineering subjects should henceforward be restricted to Years 1 and 2 of Division 2, with successful candidates then moving to the College for Years 3 and 4.

The Technological Wing

In 1906 work began on the Technological Wing, which was to house additional laboratories and practical workshops for joinery, carpentry and dyeing. The new wing was funded by grants from the Brough Trust and the SED, together with a substantial grant from the William J. Barbour Trust, set up in the name of a former Paisley businessman and the town's Liberal Member of Parliament from 1885 until his death in 1891. On completion, the new wing was officially named the Barbour Wing. Money from the Barbour Trust had also gone towards a new building for Paisley Grammar School, officially called the Paisley Grammar School and W. J. Barbour Academy.

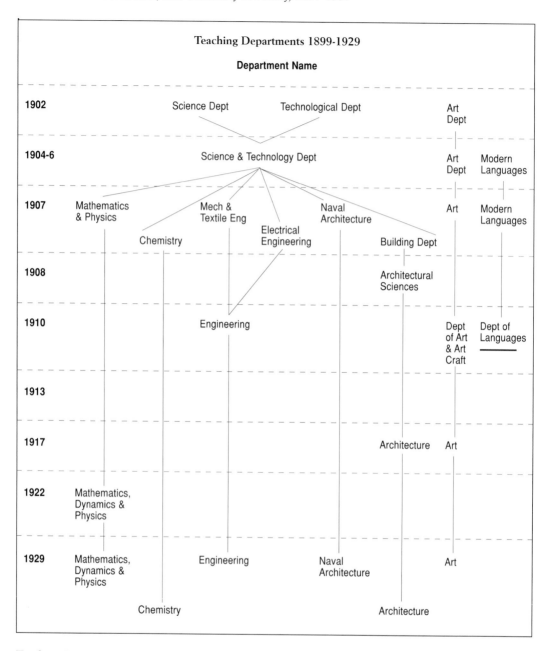

Teaching Departments 1899-1929

The cost of the Barbour Wing was estimated at £3,600 but the actual cost came to £6,195. The College's financial problems had by this time become so acute that it withdrew from the Association of Technical Institutions in order to save the cost of the subscription, and was only able to rejoin the Association when three Governors offered to pay the subscription.

Despite its problems, the College continued to expand. In 1903 the Science Department became the Science and Technology Department, and there were later sub-divisions into a Chemistry Department and a Mathematics and Physics Department in 1906. In the same year Modern Languages became a department in its own right, there also being the creation of a separate Building Department (which became Architectural Science in 1907). In that year, too, Mechanical and Textile Engineering, Electrical Engineering and Naval Architecture all appeared in the curriculum.

Funding

The setting up in 1908 of the Education (Scotland) Fund, a comprehensive source of Government financing for public education, ended the Town Council's annual funding for the College and caused another complication. It must have been humiliating for the Board of Governors, who had been fighting for CI status, to be informed that as the County Education Committee interpreted the new Fund ruling, they could not give any grant aid to the College unless it was affiliated to an appropriate CI – a view backed by the SED.

Since it was the only way to obtain funding from the County Education Committee, Principal McLean had no option but to agree most reluctantly in late 1909 to a scheme of affiliation with Glasgow and West of Scotland Technical College. Under the scheme, Paisley students who had completed Years 1 and 2 in Division 3 classes in engineering and building construction could, if they wished, transfer to the Glasgow Central Institution for their third year. At a later date the ruling was extended to include Naval Architecture. Paisley Technical College, which had earlier succeeded in taking from Camphill School the right to teach Years 3 and 4 in engineering subjects, had been hoist with its own petard.

Those students who chose to continue their studies at Paisley instead of transferring to Glasgow were free to do so, but the new situation was restrictive in that Paisley was obliged thereafter to align most of its courses with those of the Glasgow college.

An increase in the County Council's grant to £700 per annum did little to ease the College's financial problems. Internal reorganisation was essential; enrolment in art classes had decreased, and in 1909 the School of Art, which until then had had a semi-autonomous existence, was brought directly under Principal McLean's supervision and its curriculum reorganised to consist of drawing, painting, design and decorative work, and modelling and drawing from life. From then on, only drawing and painting were offered as day classes, and it was decided that embroidery and woodcarving classes would be held only if the number of applicants warranted them.

Enrolments improved slightly, but the vocational direction of the art courses lessened, and the drawing and painting classes tended to be used by ladies looking for a congenial and socially acceptable activity.

The College continued to diversify into a variety of science and industry-related courses, some leading to professional qualifications. The course on textile engineering, set up at J & P. Coats' request in 1904, was extended to include cotton spinning; its students were mainly foremen and charge-hands from the local mills.

In 1909 Principal McLean's salary was raised to £500, and the UK *Technical and Art Schools and Colleges Handbook* listed Paisley Technical College as providing courses in Mathematics and Physics, Mechanical Engineering, Textile Engineering, Naval Architecture, Electrical Engineering, Architectural Science, Sanitation, Chemistry, Dyes, Soaps, Oils and Fats, Painters' Oils, Colours and Varnishes, Food Analysis, Gas and Fuel Analysis, Water and Sewage Analysis, Pharmaceutical Chemistry, Practical Dyeing, Agricultural Science (with financial support from the County Council Education Committee), Art, Embroidery, Wood-Carving, Art Metalwork and Modern Languages.

Continuation Classes

In 1910 continuation classes in engineering, run by Johnstone, Renfrew Burgh and Renfrew Landward School Boards, were co-ordinated with Paisley Technical College, but relations between the College and the School Board remained uneasy. There were complaints that students transferring to third-year courses in the College had difficulty coping with the work, and one of the problems affecting the interaction between school and local industry was the high drop-out rate from the night-school courses.

The School of Art began to decline again, and in 1911 there was criticism within the Board of Governors about expenditure on sculpture. In this year the grant from the County Council fell from £700 to £400, though the Brough Trust increased its annual grant to £600. The College's finances were in a serious situation and a temporary loan had to be obtained from the Barbour Trust.

Exploring the problems experienced by the institution at that time, David Graham expresses the view that although proud of the College, and ambitious for it, the Board of Governors was too introverted, and local industry too lacking in ambition, to stimulate the College's situation. There was little of the civic pride and support that aided similar Colleges in areas such as Manchester, Liverpool, Sheffield and Nottingham at about the same time.

The lack of support may have had something to do with the ever-present threat of Glasgow. Paisley had survived by following the Scottish custom of 'keeping itself to itself,' and no doubt, to some members of the Board, the mere fact that Paisley had its own Technical College was enough to satisfy them.

Although the local captains of industry seemed shy of using the College's facilities to the full, they all, particularly the Coats family, continued to be generous with their gifts to the institution.

Sir William Dunn

Born in Paisley in 1833, William Dunn began working in a local accountant's office at the age of 14, later moving to a firm of merchants and importers. He then went to South Africa to work for a firm of traders, merchants and importers, and returned to Britain in 1866 a wealthy businessman.

Although he settled in England he never forgot his Paisley roots. In 1891 he became the town's Liberal MP and in that same year he paid £4,000 for a piece of land, recently cleared of its old tenements, at Paisley Cross. In 1894 he presented the land, now known as Dunn Square, to the Burgh of Paisley to be retained as open ground and a quiet retreat, with a clear view from the High Street of the then new Town Hall.

Knighted for his achievements in 1895 by Queen Victoria, whose statue holds pride of place in Dunn Square, Sir William remained Paisley's MP until 1906.

Sir William Dunn 1833-1912. Liberal MP for Paisley 1891-1906. He presented Dunn Square to the town in 1894.

When he died in 1912, bequests from his will founded the Sir William Dunn School of Pathology at Oxford University, the School of Biochemistry at Guy's Hospital, London, and the Dunn Nutrition Unit in Cambridge. His legacies to Paisley included £2,000 to the Technical College and School of Art.

By then, the College was once again in financial straits, and had to borrow upon Sir William's £2,000, as well as obtaining a temporary loan from the Brough Trust.

School of Art

In 1912 a bitter blow was dealt to the Art School when Glasgow School of Art achieved Central Institution status and became the recognised centre of advanced work, including teacher training, in the West of Scotland. From then on any pupil showing high ability in art subjects was passed on to Glasgow. In the same year Glasgow and West of Scotland Technical College became Glasgow Royal Technical College.

An approach by the School Board, who wanted to lease the College premises during the day as a Higher Grade School in place of Camphill School, was rejected; shortly afterwards the Board formally complained to the SED that the College had broken its affiliation agreement with Camphill School. An investigation by an HMI, however, found that the fault was Camphill's, and all charges against the College were withdrawn.

Day Classes Commence

At Principal McLean's suggestion, the College began holding its own day classes in engineering, science, and modern languages, as well as classes leading to the first stage of the Pharmaceutical Society examinations.

Local industry, however, was still wary of the day-release system and in the 1912-13 session only 17 students were released from employment to attend day classes in science and engineering. When Principal McLean urged the Board to seek support from leading employers, the Governors declined to take any formal action, but authorised the Principal to negotiate with the local employers as he saw fit. Enrolment figures remained small, but the day classes continued.

In his thesis Dr Graham points out that employers' disinterest in day release classes was not confined to the Paisley area. A survey carried out by the West of Scotland Joint Committee in 1910 showed that while employers supported the principle of continuation classes, they themselves preferred to stay with their usual system of apprenticeship, leaving their employees to take evening classes on a voluntary basis. Because comparatively few youngsters were keen on the idea of embarking on a study course after a long day at work, the voluntary system did little to fill classrooms.

The Board of Governors, too, preferred to observe tradition. A suggestion from George Gardiner, head of the Chemistry Department, that research and consultancy work should be undertaken in support of local firms met with the negative reaction that Sheriff Hugh Cowan had experienced in 1892 when he made a similar suggestion regarding the testing of machinery and building materials for 'outside bodies.' In Gardiner's case, the Board decided that income generated by working with and for local industry might interfere with the College's exemption from payment of municipal and parish rates.

Baptist Church

In 1911 Sir Thomas Glen-Coats gifted the site of the old Baptist Church at the corner of Storie Street and George Street to the College. With the site, one which Professor Barr had recommended in 1890 as a worthwhile future investment, came a cheque for £250.

World War 1

With the advent in 1914 of World War 1, the bulk of Britain's young and able-bodied men went off to fight for their country. The College lost potential students and some lecturers, such as David Dunn of the Art Department, and some classes had to be suspended. In their place came short courses run for munition workers, although a request from the Ministry of Munitions for a practical course in tool-making had to be turned down because the engineering laboratories were not equipped with machine tools.

In 1916 the Governors, searching for some way to ease the College's financial problems, asked the trustees of the Dunn Estate for a permanent endowment. They were turned down, though gifts and donations kept coming in, with the Coats family still very much to the fore. In the 1916/17 Calendar mention is made of a library of standard works on science, technology and art presented to the College by James Coats Jr., while Peter Coats donated a collection of Japanese prints and James Coats provided equipment for the Art Department. The Barbour Trust made a generous donation in regard to the W.B. Barbour Technological Wing, Mr John Robertson donated hand-painted Paisley shawl designs, a carding machine for the textile department came from Howard & Bullough of Accrington, and a steam engine was donated by local businessman A.F. Craig.

However, the much-needed practical support in the form of day-release apprentices was still not forthcoming. Instead, the day classes were dependent on individual and mainly local enrolments. With no summons from local industry to contribute to industrial designs, the School of Art began to decline, switching its title from Department of Arts and Crafts back to the Department of Art.

William Bow of Bow McLachlan Shipbuilding. College Governor and benefactor.

The end of the war in 1918 saw thousands of men flooding back home, eager to catch up with interrupted apprenticeships or to equip themselves with some form of training before becoming part of the brave new world that had been promised to them. Until 1922 Paisley Technical College was involved in a scheme, encouraged and supported by the Ministry of Labour, among CIs and Technical Colleges, to run special courses for returning servicemen.

By the end of the war, the College was almost £5,000 in debt, while at the same time it was slowly but steadily growing. Thanks to Principal McLean, who was working as hard as ever, it was well regarded by His Majesty's Inspectors and its students were gaining distinctions and prizes in national examinations and competitions. In recognition of his hard work the Governors increased the Principal's salary from £500 to £700 a year.

Education (Scotland) Act, 1918

In 1918 a new Education (Scotland) Act replaced School Boards by directly elected education authorities. It also made provision for compulsory attendance up to the age of 18 at continuation classes, including day release from employment; this section, however, together with a recommendation that the school leaving age be increased to 15, was not implemented for many years.

In the same year the Scotch Education Department changed its title to the more acceptable Scottish Education Department, and took over control of all Parliamentary monies earmarked for Scottish education. Although the new education authority negotiated four places on Paisley Technical College's Board of Governors, the Board continued to be made up mainly of representatives from old-established local firms.

William Bow

William Bow, a partner in the Paisley shipbuilding and engineering company of Bow and McLachlan, was yet another well-known and respected Paisley businessman and College benefactor. During World War I he had publicly offered the sum of £500 to the first airman to bring down a Zeppelin on British soil.

In 1918 he gifted 'Dunscore', a large house in Castlehead, to the College for use as a permanent residence for the Principal. In appreciation for his generosity, the Governors made Mr Bow a Life Governor of the College, and in 1922 he became Vice President of the Board.

Extension Plans

In 1919, John Denholm, who had started working at the College in 1904 as a part-time registrar and librarian, gained a full-time appointment. Although the bulk of his duties lay in administration, he also taught mathematics and physics.

In 1920 a clerkess-typist was appointed to help with administrative duties, and in the same year the Governors, responding to the influx of students following the end of the war and mindful of the changes being brought about by the 1918 Education (Scotland) Act, decided to build an extension on the Storie Street corner site gifted by Sir Thomas Glen-Coats in 1911.

Preliminary drawings of the proposed new building included craft workshops, a textile laboratory and further accommodation for the Mechanical and Electrical Engineering Department on the ground floor, with general classrooms and improved student accommodation on the upper floors. In 1917 Ayrshire Education Committee had approached the College to ask if commercial classes could be developed; at the time a decision had been deferred until after the war, but now it was agreed in principle that if the money could be found to build the extension some of the extra classrooms would be used for commercial courses.

The cost of the extension was estimated at £4,500-£4,700, with a further £6,000-£7,000 for equipment. It was agreed that finance should be raised by a direct appeal to the large industrial firms in Paisley, Johnstone and Renfrew.

When the appeal document was issued in the autumn of 1921, J & P Coats and Clark & Co. offered contributions of £5,000 each, providing that the general response to the appeal was sufficient for the project to proceed. As ill-fortune would have it, however, the appeal coincided with a general industrial recession and, sadly, the only actual contribution came from the Paisley Equitable Co-operative Society, which contributed one guinea. The appeal was dropped.

Recession

In response to the 1920s recession, the College offered 50 free places in its day courses, partly to boost attendances, which had begun to flag, and

'Dunscore' the villa in Castlehead, Paisley which was donated to the College in 1918 by William Bow. It was used as the Principal's residence until Principal Shaw's time.

Plans of Paisley Technical School.

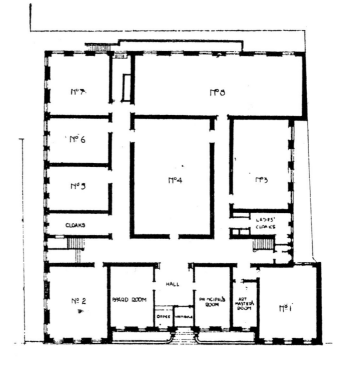

Ground floor plan of Paisley Technical School c. 1899. There were two upper floors.

GROUND FLOOR PLAN

partly as a gesture towards the local unemployment situation. It also started courses leading to external qualifications for the Associateship of the Institute of Chemistry. A class for moulders was started at the request of local iron-founders, but was closed after only two sessions due to lack of support.

Sir David Cuthbertson

Classes leading to the first part of the Pharmaceutical Society's examinations also began; the Botany lecturer on this course was biologist David Cuthbertson, at that time a young Glasgow University graduate. Later, while working in Glasgow Royal Infirmary's laboratories in the 1930s, Cuthbertson's research into the effects of post-traumatic shock led him to pioneer the use of nutrients in the treatment of seriously ill patients – important discoveries that revolutionised treatment within the world of medicine. He later became Director of the Rowett Research Institute, working on animal nutrition. A plaque was unveiled in his honour at Glasgow Royal Infirmary in January 1987.

Sir David Cuthbertson. By kind permission of the Royal Infirmary Health Board Trust.

Sir David Cuthbertson has another claim to fame outwith medicine – his son, Iain Cuthberston, is one of Scotland's best-known and respected actors.

Improved enrolments

Ex-servicemen still returning to 'civvy street' in the early 1920s brought College enrolments for the 1922/23 session to 1,353, with most of the students coming from the local catchment area. The curriculum was proving to be successful, but as so often happened when things were going well for the College, a stumbling-block appeared when the Education Authority pointed out that under the agreement made in 1909, its power to award grants to Paisley Technical College was conditional upon the affiliation of Paisley's courses with those of the Royal Technical College in Glasgow.

It seemed to the authorities that the affiliation agreement had collapsed, and while an investigation was held into the matter, the grant assistance that the Paisley College depended on so desperately was held in abeyance.

It transpired that during a reconstruction of the West of Scotland Joint Committee made necessary by the 1918 Education (Scotland) Act, Paisley Technical College's membership had been overlooked. Principal McLean had not been notified of Committee meetings for a number of years, but for some reason (possibly because he preferred to let the College look after its own affairs) he had not made any enquiries about the matter.

The affiliation was re-affirmed and the College allocated two places on the Committee, which meant that Angus McLean had, with reluctance, to oversee some re-alignment of courses which in his view had been running very well as they were.

In 1923 the special courses for returning servicemen came to an end and the continuing economic recession meant that day enrolments were considerably reduced. However, there was an increase in the numbers of female students, almost certainly brought about by some employers recognising the abilities women had shown during the war years. The art and modern language courses were popular with many of the female students, and facilities were also made available within the College for examinations of the Institute of Bankers.

The new Education Act had introduced a series of national diplomas and certificates linking education and industry more closely and creating a 'ladder' from apprenticeship to professional status. The Ordinary National Diploma (OND) required two years of full-time study and led to the Higher National Diploma (HND) which took a further year of full-time study. The Ordinary National Certificate (ONC) required three years' part-time study, and the Higher National Certificate (HNC), a further two years' part-time study, acting as a doorway to professional qualifications at degree or honours degree level.

The new courses had already been established in England, but when the SED suggested their introduction into Paisley Technical College in 1924, Principal McLean rejected the idea, possibly because such an agreement could, as had happened with the affiliation with a Central Institution, open the door to decisions being made by authorities outwith the College about its courses.

Semi-Jubilee

In 1926 the College celebrated its semi-Jubilee. A students' dance in Paisley Town Hall was attended by Principal McLean and his wife and daughter, the Reverend John Porteous, BD, Chairman of the Board of Governors, and his family, and a number of local dignitaries and benefactors.

Reporting the event, a *Paisley and Renfrewshire Gazette* editorial commented, 'The Technical College's success constitutes a remarkable triumph over difficulties, for it was inaugurated amid an atmosphere of scepticism and fear, and only steady determination and sound teaching, plus the interest of strong personalities, have brought it to the high state of efficiency and importance which it today occupies.'

'Scepticism and fear' seems harsh, but it was certainly true that the College's survival was a triumph over difficulties. Finance was an ongoing problem, and every penny had to be accounted for. In his booklet, *90 Years of Degree Teaching in Chemistry*, written in 1991, Alastair Mitchell, of the Chemistry Department, recalls this reminder to students in 1920. 'All common reagents will be provided, but they must be used economically, and no unnecessary waste of chemicals, gas or water will be allowed. Students will be held responsible for any breakages which occur through their carelessness, and a deposit of five shillings (25p) is required. . . .'

It should be pointed out at this stage that there has been uncertainty in the past as to the date of the University's official anniversaries. Those who authorised the semi-Jubilee clearly took their lead from 1900, when the Duke of Argyll formally opened the Technical School, and since then others have followed the same path. But the decision has now been made that the most important date on the College/University calendar should be November 30th, 1897, the day the foundation stone was laid.

As it happens, Peter Brough, the man behind the original formation of the Technical School, was born in 1797, which means that the University's official centenary, 1997, coincides with the bi-centenary of his birth.

The Bow Bequest

When William Bow, the shipbuilder who had donated the Principal's residence in 1918, died in 1927, he left a bequest of £25,000 to the College, with a proviso that half of the money should go towards the establishment of classes in costing and general accountancy, book-keeping, Spanish and French. The legacy must have caused Governors and Principal alike to believe that at last their financial problems were to be eased, but once again fate intervened. Because of litigation the bequest, when it was eventually released to the College, fell far short of the original sum and William Bow's wishes could not be implemented.

In his thesis, Dr David Graham notes that after Mr Bow's demise, Thomas White, of the engineering company T. White & Sons, seems to have been the only local industrialist to try periodically to rouse the Governors from the torpor which had gripped them since the war. Mr White also gifted equipment to the College from time to time and persuaded others to do the same.

Continued Prejudice against Day-Release.

Although Lord Eustace Percy, President of the Board of Education 1924-1929, was keen to see technical education linked more closely to industry, his own Board's Committee on Education and Industry, together with an SED committee, reported in 1928 that employers still preferred voluntary evening classes to day-release classes.

Paisley College had a similar experience when it approached J & P Coats with a proposal for day-release arrangements for the firm's apprentices. A spokesman for the company raised various difficulties and the proposal was eventually turned down. In 1926 however, the College began a course for external qualifications for the Institute of Textiles, and in 1927 came a course leading to external qualifications in Sanitary Science for the Board of Health.

The fortunes of industry, local and country-wide, had fluctuated throughout the 1920s; now, on the threshold of the 1930s, the first cold winds of what was to be a crippling depression began to blow. College enrolment figures, which had been steadily rising, began to decrease. Improved accommodation and equipment were badly needed, but resources were already stretched to the full extent of their capacity, even though in

1929 Paisley soap-manufacturer and Liberal MP Sir James McCallum left a bequest of £3,000 to the College in his will.

Angus McLean

In 1929, after giving 30 years of service to the College, Principal Angus McLean announced his retirement.

From the time he had taken on the Principal's post, he had been fired with ambition for the School/College, and had admirably fulfilled his duties as set down in the Governors' advertisement. He had introduced the London University External Degree examinations and played his part in establishing the College as a reputable centre of higher education.

Acting as College Secretary and Treasurer, J & A. Gardner's law firm in County Place kept the books as well as administering and paying out salaries. Communication between the College and the office was conducted by post and, says Miss Margaret White, who worked in the Gardner offices from 1926, 'you also used your two legs.' She recalls Angus McLean as 'a gently spoken man, a real Highlandman.'

To mark his retiral, the Governors presented him with a five-valve portable wireless and gramophone set, and a substantial cheque. His steady hand had been on the helm since the very beginning. Now the search was on for an able replacement.

Chapter 3
Principal Lewis Fry Richardson
(1929-1940)

Lewis Fry Richardson was undoubtedly the most distinguished Principal in the College's hundred-year history. Born in Newcastle and educated at the city's Durham College of Science and King's College Cambridge, he graduated from Cambridge with first-class honours in 1903 and worked as an assistant at the National Physical Laboratory, then in an electric lamp factory before taking up a post with the Meteorological Office.

In 1926 he was made a Fellow of the Royal Society, one of the highest scientific honours in the country.

When the Meteorological Office was placed under the jurisdiction of the Air Ministry in 1920, Richardson, a Quaker and a pacifist who had served with the Friends' Ambulance Unit in France during World War 1, resigned his post on conscientious grounds. He joined the staff of Westminster Training College as Head of the Physics Department, moving from there to Paisley on October 1st 1929, with a salary of £1,000 per annum.

Principal Richardson.

The new Principal took over at a time when College accommodation was inadequate, London University was complaining about the lack of facilities available for Paisley students studying for its external examinations, and attempts to provide more buildings had fallen through.

What the College needed just then was a shrewd administrator with the ability to steer it through the stormy waters of the 1930s Depression and to find solutions for its financial problems. What it got was a brilliant academic whose interest lay in research rather than in teaching and administration.

Dr Richardson's biographer, Oliver M Ashford, writes in *Prophet or Professor? – The Life and Work of Lewis Fry Richardson* that Richardson converted a large room at Dunscore, his official residence, into a study/laboratory, and a smaller room into a chemical and photographic laboratory.

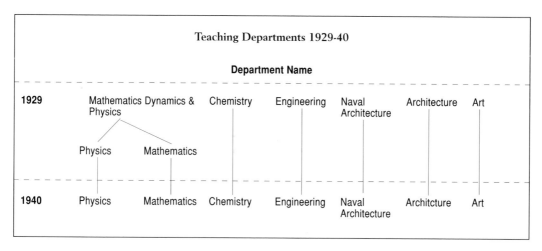

Teaching Departments 1929-40

Department Name

1929	Mathematics Dynamics & Physics	Chemistry	Engineering	Naval Architecture	Architecture	Art
	Physics Mathematics					
1940	Physics Mathematics	Chemistry	Engineering	Naval Architecture	Architcture	Art

Teaching Departments 1929-40

Not long after taking up his post in Paisley he indicated to the Governors that he was not prepared to take on the teaching load that his predecessor had carried. Angus McLean had taught for 38 hours per week on top of his duties as Principal, but Dr Richardson considered that the 16 hours a week he gave to teaching evening classes, in addition to working all day, was 'unusually much, personally disagreeable, and not for the good of the College.'

The College did benefit, though, from some of the new Principal's innovations. Richardson introduced teaching to Ordinary and Higher Certificate standards, a move which his predecessor had rejected and which opened up the way to future developments. At first the Certificate courses were taught in Mechanical Engineering, Electrical Engineering, Naval Architecture and Chemistry, with an ONC course in Building included later.

A year before moving to Paisley, Dr Richardson, a man who thirsted after knowledge all his life, had taken the London University External Honours Degree in Psychology. The introduction in Paisley College in 1931 of an evening course in Psychology came about through his interest in the subject. The lecturer appointed to teach Industrial Psychology was Charles Oakley, author of several histories of Glasgow, including *The Second City*. He subsequently taught Industrial Psychology at Glasgow University.

Although relieved of teaching the most elementary classes after his protest, the Principal continued of his own accord to maintain a routine which involved working all day, then returning to the College after an evening meal and a brief nap to teach physics and mathematics up to the standard required for the London external degree. When, under the National Economy Act, staff members of further education colleges suffered an $8\frac{1}{3}$% cut in their salaries in 1931, L.F. Richardson presented a paper to the Board of Governors, comparing Paisley with other colleges throughout the UK and proving that he and his full-time Heads of Departments carried a heavier teaching load than any of their counterparts.

Two years later a further cut of 1⅔% was made in the salaries of the Principal and full-time lecturers.

Money was always tight. Giving the Principal permission to represent Paisley at meetings of the Association of Technical Institutions early in 1931, the Governors decided that he should travel third class. An appeal made at the time for a new galvanometer reads, 'A high bicycle dating from 1890 may be in perfect condition, but one would not like to be seen riding it on the road. Similarly, a galvanometer of Kelvin's first type may be in perfect condition, but modern galvanometers are so much more convenient. . . .'

Just three months after Richardson's arrival, Paisley was dealt a punishing blow. Scottish tradition demands that every house should be spotlessly clean to welcome the new year; on Hogmanay (New Year's Eve) of 1929 the children's matinee at the Glen Cinema at Paisley Cross was filled with youngsters who had been dispatched from home so that their mothers could get on with the housework.

During the matinee a reel of film in the projection room caught alight. The incident in itself was trivial, but when smoke from the burning film filtered into the auditorium, the children panicked and made a rush for the exits which, on that day, were locked. Sixty-nine children were crushed and smothered to death before rescuers could get to them.

The Glen Cinema. By kind permission of the *Glasgow Herald*.

On the first Ne'erday (New Year's Day) Dr Richardson and his wife

Dorothy spent in Paisley, there were none of the usual festivities. Instead, the town, in mourning for its dead children, moved silently into what was to be known as the Hungry Thirties.

Hard pressed though it was, the College, as it had in the 1920s, did what it could to offer an alternative to unemployment in the 1930s. Principal Richardson offered free places in industrial-based day and evening classes to unemployed men, the only condition being that those who took up the offer did so as a serious commitment. Fees were kept low for other students, and bursaries were made available from the Brough Trust and other sources to help those who wanted to learn.

Financial Problems and the Need for Expansion

In 1931 the Board of Governors asked Renfrew County Council for the use of the disused part of the Central School in nearby George Street to ease the accommodation problem. Their request was granted, but the premises were in such poor condition, bringing a flurry of complaints from students and employers alike, that the College had to abandon all thought of using them.

In 1933 London University renewed its formal recognition of Paisley Technical College as an approved centre, but only for a four-year term instead of the usual six years, and on condition that improvements would be made in specialist accommodation and equipment. They also requested what amounted to the appointment of an additional member of staff in the Engineering Department. While their recognition proved that the College was a good teaching centre, the time restriction indicated that the lack of finances was seriously crippling its advancement.

At the request of the Renfrew firm of Babcock & Wilcox, a course of arc welding was introduced, only to be discontinued after its first session because of lack of support. The day was to come, however, when the Renfrew company and Paisley Technical College would forge strong links.

In 1934, it began to look as though the day release clause in the 1918 Education (Scotland) Act was about to be implemented at last; indeed, it was believed that an estimated £12m was being made available nationally for the scheme.

By then the College badly needed an expansion programme, having used up every inch of available space. During the 1920s, two corridor areas had been enclosed to provide two extra lecture rooms and a cloakroom had to be turned into an art room. Since 1931, the Governors' board-room had doubled as a staff-room, while the original staff-room became a lecture room. A photographic darkroom had to be used as a part-time lecture room, and offers of a loom, which would have been of great benefit to the weaving class, and two demonstration motor chassis from the Ford Motor Company had to be turned down because of lack of floor-space.

Plans had been revived for a modest extension built on land purchased at Townhead Terrace, but after a discussion with the chief HMI, Principal Richardson, under the mistaken impression that the College's share of the

The piecemeal expansion of the College buildings between 1900 and the 1940s took place largely on the site of the former dyeworks which had used the (by then culverted) St Mirren Burn. The land and buildings were donated or sold to the College by Coats. All of the extensions to the Gardner Building have since been demolished.

1. The first extension was completed in 1906 and was known as the 'Barbour' or 'Technological' Wing. It incorporated parts of the old dyeworks; included engineering labs and workshops, and was funded by the Brough and Barbour Trusts. It was described in the 1950s as a 'warren'.
2. In 1911 Thomas Glen-Coats donated the site of a former Baptist Church at the corner of George Street and Storie Street. A public appeal for funds to build on this site was abandoned in 1921 and temporary buildings were subsequently erected.
3. The 'Bow Wing', including Chemistry labs and other facilities requested by London University for external students, was the result of Principal Richardson's negotiations throughout the 1930s. It was built between 1938 and 1940 and survived until the 1960s.

There was a janitor's house in the buildings to the west of the main block and the College also owned 'Dunscore', the Principal's residence in Castlehead, donated by William Bow.

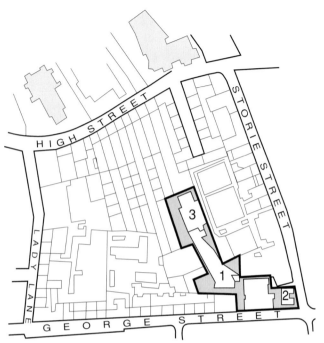

The College Buildings 1900-1940

£12m would be considerable, began to think along more ambitious lines. He had been advised that as well as meeting its own immediate needs, the College should also aim to provide for the introduction of trades classes – something that the Governors had always resisted.

As Dr David Graham points out in his thesis, further consultation with the SED would have shown Dr Richardson that his estimate of both Scotland's, and Paisley's, share of the £12m. was in error, but instead of seeking confirmation, the Principal started working out two alternative expansion plans. In 1936 the Board of Governors approved the preparation of a further extension scheme, and accepted the provision for trades classes.

Following the Governors' approval, there was consultation with the education authority regarding the numbers of apprentices in existing local trades and the numbers of students in continuation classes in Camphill Secondary School and other local centres. Plans were then prepared for a substantial extension at an estimated total cost of £100,000, plus the cost of a site to the west of the College, to be bought from J & P. Coats.

Sadly, when the scheme was submitted to the SED, they pointed out that as the College was not a Central Institution they could only provide up to 50% of the estimated cost (and even that would only be possible under a special minute) on condition that the £50,000 balance could be raised locally. Then came more bad news – J & P Coats wanted £3,000 for their land, while the Governors were only prepared to offer £500 for what they considered to be 'point six of an acre, covering an old pond.'

Even although in 1935 Lady McCallum, widow of Sir James McCallum, left a legacy of £2,000 in her will, the College had no hope of raising the sum required for the ambitious expansion plan. It had to be abandoned in favour of a modest extension to the Barbour Wing, and even that, if London University's requirements were to be met, would cost almost £10,000. The SED eventually agreed to support the project on a 50% of cost basis under the Education (Scotland) Paisley Technical College and School of Art Special Grant Regulation of 1938.

The Coats Connection

Major Harold Glen-Coats' death in 1934 left the Board of Governors without a member of the Coats family for the first time since its inauguration. From then on the family was represented on the Board by a member of J & P Coats' managerial staff.

Joseph McLean OBE, and Stuart Emery MBE

Among those students who took advantage of the College's offer of higher education in the 1930s were Joseph McLean, the son of a local tradesman, and Stuart Emery, who had been educated at Johnstone High School and Camphill High School in Paisley, ending his formal education at the age of fifteen.

The first member of his family to enter further education, Joseph McLean began his studies in 1932, and after completing his course in 1936, he followed what had already become College tradition by returning as a part-time staff member from 1938-1940. He then joined the full-time staff and eventually became Head of the Chemistry Department from 1945 to 1974. Joseph McLean retired in 1974 and died in 1987. In the late 1960s while he was in charge there were over six hundred Chemistry students and twenty-seven full time staff.

Stuart Emery, an apprentice draughtsman at Clifton & Baird's engineering firm in Johnstone, found that not all the students who started the courses were dedicated enough to study from 7-10 p.m., especially if they had just completed a full day's work. He recalls that there could be anything up to 100-120 students in a class at the beginning of a course; the number dwindled over the following 3-4 years until only six or seven remained to sit the final examinations.

Mr Emery, one of the 'stayers,' recalls that most of the evening lecturers came from local industry and 'were all very highly qualified'. After taking his HNC in Mechanical Engineering with distinction in all subjects, he went on to study at the Glasgow Royal College, where he again did well. He passed all the exams necessary to become a member of the Institution of Mechanical Engineers, only to discover that he was still too young to become a full member. Eventually, age prevailed, and he became a Fellow of the Institution.

During the Second World War Mr Emery, in a reserved occupation, was persuaded by his former Paisley lecturer, Alex McCrorie, to join him

I have known people do badly in examinations for diverse reasons : —

A. Those not provided by nature with a suitable apparatus inside the skull. With regard to them it is well to remember the dictum of Spearman, the eminent psychologist, "everyone is a genius at some-thing"

B. Those who have not learnt enough, either because of short time, enforced interruptions, but usually because of pleasant distractions.

C. Those who think of an examination as a test of knowledge only. Whereas examiners regard it as a test partly of knowledge, but also of ability to think about rather novel unexpected situations. Candidates in this class c spend the week before the examination in feverishly stuffing information into a mind already full; they arrive at the examination tired, unable to think clearly about anything unexpected; all they can do is to pour out what they have learnt; and in so doing they are too fatigued to notice whether it is really relevant. They remind me of the man who was betted that he couldn't drink a bucketful of beer, and just before trying in public, did it privately to make sure that he could.

Principal Richardson's view on why students fail exams. (Richardson Notebooks Vol 1, p 337.)

58

in the design office of a Glasgow machine-tool company and to become a part-time lecturer at Paisley Technical College. A year later he returned to Clifton & Baird as Works Manager, working his way up to Managing Director. Eventually he and his family bought the company.

His interest in education and training led to an involvement with the Paisley and Johnstone Training Group, where he became Chairman for 21 years and also Chairman of all Scottish Training Groups. In 1976 he became a Governor of Paisley College of Technology, and in 1995, when he was Chairman of Governors, a block of student accommodation in Christie Street was formally named Emery House in honour of his links with the College (by then the University of Paisley) as a student, lecturer and employer.

Students such as Stuart Emery and Joseph McLean proved that a combination of work training and further education can take an ambitious youngster far.

The College in the late 1930s

In 1938, the year when Tait's Tower soared high above Glasgow's Empire Exhibition in Bellahouston Park, work began on the Barbour Wing extension, with parts of the Bow and McCallum legacies meeting the College's share of the cost. It was named the Bow Wing. In the same year Governor Thomas White, of the Paisley firm of Thomas White & Son, suggested the setting up of Standing Committees of the Board of Governors to cover Finance and Salaries, Appointments, and Premises and Equipment, all of which were being dealt with largely by the Principal and his Registrar, John Denholm. Mr White was invited to prepare a scheme which, when presented to the Governors, was remitted back for further consideration.

In the late 1930s Scotland's first industrial estate had been set up at Hillington, between Paisley and Glasgow. Created by the Scottish Economic Committee under the Scottish Development Council, the estate marked the start of a planned approach to regional industrial development which, it was hoped, could result in benefits to technical colleges such as Paisley's.

The College auditors, consulted in the on-going search for ways of cost-saving, advised the curtailment of non-grant-earning facilities and the discontinuation of low-enrolment classes. They also recommended an increase in fees and a re-examination of the level of staff remunerations. However, their suggestions like Mr White's scheme for Standing Committees, and the proposed development of regional industry marked by the Hillington Industrial Estate, were all suspended towards the end of 1939, when Europe found itself entering upon a second world war.

L.F. Richardson

In February 1940, Principal Lewis Fry Richardson, then aged 58, announced his retirement. The reason given was that he needed more time to carry out research into the instability of peace, and his biographer, Oliver M. Ashford, believes that this was so. Although the subject closest to

Dr Richardson's heart was meteorological physics, he had become increasingly absorbed during the 1930s in the pursuit of peace in the world, publishing *Mathematical Psychology of War* in 1935 and *Generalised Foreign Politics* in 1939.

The general belief in the University to this day, however, is that his sudden decision was due, in part at least, to training classes held in the College during the war years in wireless and radio for military personnel. The classes did not begin until well after the Principal's retirement, but Hamish MacLachlan, the College's first Librarian, understood that when war first broke out, Dr Richardson had refused to allow the premises to be used for such training. It may be that he knew that the introduction of such classes would eventually be forced on the College.

At the discretion of the Governors, Dr Richardson and his wife remained in the official residence for a further three years before moving to Kilmun in Argyll, where he died in 1953.

The *Dictionary of National Biography* (1951-1960) says of him that research was, '. . . the inevitable consequence of the tendency of his mental machine to run almost, but not quite, of itself. So he was a bad listener, distracted by his thoughts, and a bad driver, seeing his dream instead of the traffic. . . .'

Although he worked at the Meteorological Office for only four years in all, Lewis Fry Richardson was the pioneer of numerical weather forecasting, and considered by the Met Office to be the most famous scientist to have

'I feel that I must make time to prosecute thoroughly researches on the instability of peace . . .' Principal Richardson's letter of resignation as included in the Minute of the Board of Governor's meeting held on 28th February 1940.

Dear Sirs,

I feel that I must make time to prosecute thoroughly researches on the Instability of Peace in continuation of my recent book called "Generalized Foreign Politics" (Camb. Un. Press 1939). Accordingly I hereby give notice to leave the service of the Governors three months hence, that is on May 16th. I have chosen that date because then I will just have finished the evening classes which I teach personally.

I wish to thank yourselves and the Governors for courtesy and consideration during the 10½ years that I have lived in Paisley.

Yours faithfully,
(Signed) Lewis F. Richardson.

Theory of the Rainbow   20

Winklemann's Physik 2te Aufl Optik p 1089.

Classed under the "Diffraction of Non-Spherical Waves"
The first rainbow was explained by Descartes by a single
internal reflection, leading to a minimum of deviation;
the second rainbow by a double internal reflection leading
to a maximum of deviation. But in addition there
are numerous subsidiary rings which can only be
explained by diffraction.

Considering only one internal reflexion. ~~before~~ Parallel
light incident. The refraction & reflexion leads to the following

Incident light strikes drop	angle of incidence	angle of reflexion	Deviation D	Remarks
centrally			180°	
grazingly			166° = D'	
	$\sin i = \frac{1}{\sqrt{3}}(4-n^2)$		$\pi+2i-4r = \bar{D}$ 137° 40' to 139° 40' in visible range	D a minimum.

next the diffraction modifies the position of greatest
intensity which for small drops does not correspond to the
minimum of D. Thus for drops of 2 mm diameter the
maximum intensity occurs at a deviation 12' less than the
minimum. For drops of 0·02 mm diam, at 4° less than the
minimum deviation & the general formula is that if
a be the radius of the drop and if λ be the wave length
of light, then the bow of maximum intensity has a
deviation less than the minimum deviation by approximately
$$0·507\left(\frac{\lambda}{a}\right)^{2/3}$$

OVER

A page from L.F. Richardson's Notebook held in the University Library Archive. (Vol 2, p 210)

(5). As to air-raid precautions against poison gas I feel that A.R.P. wardens should have the habit of observing (i) katabatic winds (ii) the dispersal of smoke; also that the (ARP) Head-quarters of a town like Paisley (90,000 population) should know about lapse-rates. So I asked leave of the police (who control A.R.P. here) to give a lecture on turbulence. They were at first re-luctant, but finally permitted me to address the Gas Identifications Officers (G.I.O.), who are learned chemists. The G.I.O. listened very politely. I offered to lend them a lapse-rate meter; but that they politely declined. It is not aspirated unfortunately, yet it is better protected against radiation than some ~~folk~~ (meteorologists) might imagine. Naturally the local A.R.P. authorities take their tone from national headquarters. I guess that they regard turbulence, lapse-rates, and all that, as little more than a personal hobby of a retired local resident.

yours faithfully Lewis F. Richardson.

Extract from a letter written by L F Richardson dated 26 November 1942.
(Richardson Papers Vol 2, p 277).

worked there. In October 1972 the Richardson Wing, which houses the Met Office's central Forecast Office and computer sections, was officially opened by the Rt. Hon. Edward Heath, then Prime Minister. A sad irony lies in the fact that although Dr Richardson resigned because the Met Office became part of the Air Ministry, the Richardson Wing lies within a Ministry of Defence complex. The Office holds a vast amount of literature by and about Dr Richardson, and in May 1993 celebrated the publication of his collected papers.

The Royal Meteorological Society instituted the annual L. F. Richardson Prize in 1960, and a Centre for Conflict Resolution in London was named the Richardson Institute in 1969. In 1965 the Richardson Institute for Peace Studies was founded at the newly established Lancaster University, the first British university formally to include the study of peace research.

Some people who came in contact with Richardson during his time as Principal of Paisley Technical College found him difficult to fathom. Stuart Emery recalls one occasion when, while he was there in the 1930s as a student, mathematics lecturer Alex McCrorie was ill and Principal Richardson took charge of the classroom. 'He filled the board with calculus a good wee bit beyond anything we had then got to. He was very much like the absent-minded professor.'

Claud McNeil, a student from 1935-1941, and later a College lecturer, remembers Dr Richardson as 'a very practical man in the laboratory. He

never lectured – he just wrote on the blackboard, or he would come in and say, "I've been puzzling over this equation all afternoon. . . ." and write it on the board, then say, "I'll go away – see what you can make of it." We couldn't even understand the symbols!'

Mr McNeil didn't endear himself to the Principal when Dr Richardson entrusted him with the stop-watch which was his 'pride and joy,' so that he could time an experiment on a heated syrup solution. Unfortunately, Mr McNeil dropped the watch into the syrup. Dr Richardson, he recalls, was livid.

Dr Richardson's technician in many of the experiments he set up in the College was Charlie Alford,

Claud McNeil

described by Arthur Hughes, a College technician between 1957 and 1987, as 'the finest craftsman I have ever met . . . Charlie could use a hacksaw like a precision surgeon.'

As Dr David Graham points out in his thesis, there was a side to Principal Richardson that the students did not see. As has been said, he defended his staff during salary cuts, and James Denholm, Joseph McLean and Margaret MacNab, the first woman to work in the College office, all thought highly of his kindliness, integrity and intellect. Discovering that Miss MacNab was on a low salary, Dr Richardson insisted that she be given her first increase in ten years, and he also introduced the practice of listing non-academic staff, hitherto ignored, in the College Calendars.

He is remembered, too, for his inventiveness in the laboratories, where he had a great talent, not only for developing experiments, but also for devising the apparatus and equipment to carry them out.

A keen runner, he was often to be seen jogging around the Paisley streets early in the morning, in shorts and vest. On one occasion he happened to jog past one of the mills when the girls were coming off duty and was forced, for the sake of his dignity, to increase his pace when a number of them started running behind him.

Dedicated academic though he was, L.F. Richardson possessed a strong sense of humour. Oliver Ashford reports in his biography that he was fond of playing pranks on fellow students in his younger days, and Claud McNeil recalls that when Ralph Richardson, the Principal's nephew and one of Britain's greatest twentieth century actors, appeared in a play in the Paisley Theatre, his uncle sat in the front row making faces in an attempt to break the young actor's concentration.

An article in *The Guardian* in April 1993, 'Weather Watcher on the Western Front', by John and Mary Gribbin describes him as 'a man ahead of his time,' and points out that L. F. Richardson died too soon to see his mathematical system of forecasting weather patterns reach fruition because

An apparatus for absolute resistance determination using bicycle wheels and a solenoid. A page from Principal Richardson's notebooks in the Library archives. (Vol 21, p 198)

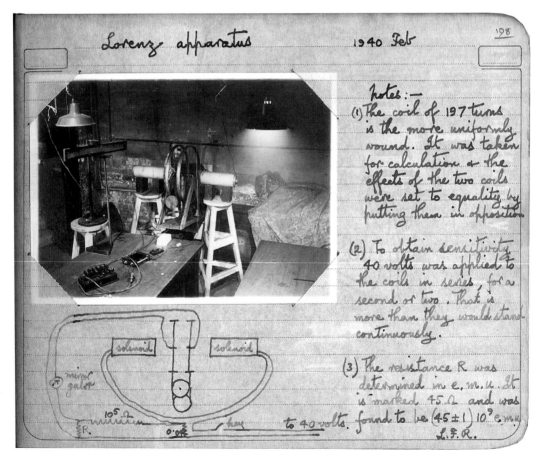

his theories, originated in the 1920s, could not be put into use until the development thirty years later of the electronic computer. The article goes on to say that L. F. Richardson 'possessed one of the most able, original and versatile minds ever devoted to meteorology. . . .'

Many have wondered why a man of Lewis Fry Richardson's stature took up an appointment at a small technical college in the first place. The answer is thought to lie in the man's unswerving beliefs as a Quaker and a pacifist, which may have led him to make decisions which did not help his academic career.

Dr. Richardson and Paisley Technical College were, perhaps, not entirely suited to each other but conversely, the very fact that they were unsuited adds to his importance in the University's history. He could be compared to the pearl in the College's oyster shell; just as the pearl starts life as an irritation which, after being covered with layers of mother-of-pearl, emerges as a valuable gem, so the mere fact that for eleven years Lewis Fry Richardson was within its walls has added lustre to the University's status.

Chapter 4
Acting Principal John Denholm
(1940-1946)

Acting Principal Denholm.

Following L.F. Richardson's sudden resignation, the Board of Governors appointed the College Registrar, John Denholm, to the post of Acting Principal. He was sixty-three years of age when he took up his new duties in May 1940.

Born in Berwickshire, John Denholm had served his apprenticeship by working as a pupil-teacher; although he had no formal training, let alone a degree, he did well in his chosen profession, and in 1904, not long after settling with his family in Paisley, he had been appointed part-time Registrar in the College, a position that became full-time in 1919. He also taught physics. His son James was a day-student, studying for a London University external degree.

War Years

John Denholm became Acting Principal at a time when, as had happened at the beginning of the Great War, enrolments had dropped sharply. As SED funding was calculated on a per capita basis, fewer enrolments meant lower grant funding and further financial hardships at a time when London University was warning once again that the lack of practical facilities and levels of equipment at Paisley would have to improve. Day classes were being taught by a skeleton staff, and for the first four war years, attendance at evening classes was restricted by the number of places available in the College's air-raid shelter.

There is still an area within the George Street building marked Air Raid Shelter. Stuart Emery, who passed his 6th year exams in 1941 and became a part-time evening teacher the following year, recalls an examination being hurriedly abandoned when the sirens were heard. 'Everyone went down into the dungeon. The shelter was warm and stuffy, sandbagged and not comfortable. There was a labyrinth of corridors . . . I don't know what they would have done if the College had come down on top of us.'

He also remembers walking home after evening classes with lecturers Alex McCrorie and Sam Hosie on the night of the Clydebank blitz, and '. . . dodging in and out of closes as the German bombers droned overhead.'

Donald Stevenson, who commenced evening classes at the College in 1940/41, remembers the dangers caused by the blackout. 'If you ran out of the building too quickly after classes, you could trip over the big pipes laid along the George Street gutters. They had something to do with the water supplies, in case of fires.'

Donald, who eventually became a Senior Lecturer in the Chemistry Department (and in 1997 is still helping with the administration of the CATS Scheme), worked in the laboratory at the Royal Ordnance Factory in Bishopton during the war. He was on shift work, which made

The entrance to the College air raid shelter still visible at the rear of 'G' Block.

it difficult, at times, for him to keep up with his evening classes. 'Day shift wasn't too bad but it wasn't easy when I was on the early shift (when I had to get up at 4.30 a.m.) or the night shift. It was a pretty hard slog – working, going to class, taking notes, and sleeping.

'The College was a very busy place when I first began attending classes. There was a lot of activity in the evenings, and of course there were the training classes for radar technicians, taken by Jim Denholm.

'The Physics class for the London degree was in the furthest away room in the Bow Wing, past the boiler house, through the old dye-works, and right towards the back door.' John Denholm took the class, which began with about 20 students, but dwindled in time to about six.

Work on the Bow Wing had been completed shortly after the outbreak of war. Ronald Scott, who began studying full-time for the London external degree in 1942, recalls, 'All we had then was the building in George Street . . . there were also a whole lot of single-storey brick-built buildings that wandered over the area and housed the labs. Virtually all the lecturers were in the main building.'

There were only about 15 full-time students in Mr Scott's matriculation class, and so few in some subjects that 'it was almost individual tuition.' In 1943 only one student was doing a final year BSc in Engineering. The London Matriculation involved English as a required subject; it was taught by a teacher from Camphill School in a three-hour session every Saturday morning.

'The London external degrees gave Paisley prestige,' Mr Scott says. 'There were very few art students at that time. I only recall one female student, and she was in the Art School.

'In those early days the place was stiff with soldiers, being taught electrical engineering as far as we could make out, probably training for radar. Teachers such as physics teachers were taken from the secondary schools to teach them.'

One of those teachers was John Denholm's son James who, after graduating, taught physics in Camphill School by day and evening classes at the College. When war broke out he was seconded to MT5 under the War Office, and moved to the College to set up and run electronic classes for service personnel, mainly Canadians. Twenty-eight years later in an interview in IMPACT, the student magazine, he was to recall, 'for almost six years I struggled with the enemy, Canadians and the War Office.'

Though Clydebank, some 5 miles to the north, and Greenock, about 20 miles to the west, were badly bombed, Paisley itself escaped relatively unscathed. It suffered only one major tragedy, but even so it was one too many. One night in May 1941, a landmine drifted down towards the town at the end of a parachute. Had the parachute been blown in a different direction, the mine might well have landed and exploded in Woodside Cemetery but instead, the wind guided it away from the cemetery to drop onto Woodside First-Aid Post, filled at the time with doctors, nurses, ambulance personnel and helpers. It was a direct hit, and soon afterwards, a second landmine hit part of the nearby West School, in use as an auxiliary fire station. In all, 92 Paisley folk were killed.

In November 1943, Paisley Grammar School was almost gutted by a fire. Until it was rebuilt the senior classes were taught in College accommodation. The Board of Governors met only 16 times during the six war years, one occasion being in April 1942, when John Denholm reached retirement age and the Board extended his appointment as temporary Principal.

When the special classes for service personnel ended in 1945, a total of 580 having taken the courses, John Denholm persuaded his son to remain at the College on a full-time basis instead of returning to Camphill School. Later, James Denholm was to say of his decision, 'A return to the rather humdrum life of a school was not very attractive, and at the request of my father, and without any financial inducement whatever, I chose to engage with him in rescuing the College from its rather desperate situation. I had become used to challenges and relished the opportunity of further adventure.'

Admiral Sir Lindsay Bryson

One of the many students affected by the war was Lindsay Bryson, who, on gaining the matriculation requirements required for a London University

Admiral Sir Lindsay Bryson, President of the Institution of Electrical Engineers 1985-86.

external degree at night-school, became a full-time student at Paisley Technical College in the early 1940s.

After a few terms, the young student, his savings almost gone, gained a place on a cadetship scheme aimed at training engineers for the Services. He continued to attend the College in the evenings, passing the intermediate BSc and Part 1 of the finals. His interest had switched by then from civil to electrical engineering, and in 1945 he joined the Navy as an electrical mechanic. Over the following nine years, studying when and where he could, he gained a 1st-class external BSc degree from London University.

In 1983, Sir Lindsay became the first electrical engineer to achieve the rank of Admiral. He was elected as Honorary Fellow of the IEE in 1991, and served as President of the Institution 1985-86.

Frank J. Phillips OBE

Until the 1940s there had been little contact between the College and the large Renfrew factory of Babcock & Wilcox, other than the discarded course on arc welding in the 1930s. Supplying a boiler to the College in 1940, Babcocks had generously written off £505 from the cost as their contribution to the Barbour Wing extension fund.

Frank J Phillips OBE (1895-1965) as depicted in GESA in May 1953. Mr Phillips was Chief Education Officer for Babcocks and Wilcox and Chairman of the Board of Governors 1950-1960.

In 1945, Frank J. Phillips, invalided out of the RAF because of war wounds, became Chief Education Officer for Babcock and Wilcox, and formed the company's Education Department. Renfrew division was their main UK apprenticeship base and Phillips, working closely with a number of universities and colleges, came to an agreement with Acting Principal John Denholm which resulted in Babcock trainees and apprentices attending Paisley Technical College. The joint decision opened up an important new partnership which was to be of mutual benefit.

The first Babcock and Wilcox employee to be co-opted onto the College's Board of Governors, Phillips was enthusiastic about Paisley's ability to teach the London University external degree course in engineering, for it meant that Babcock and Wilcox employees could keep up their studies at degree level, whether at home or abroad.

Accommodation Problems

Welcome though the sudden increase in student numbers caused by the Babcock influx was, it emphasised the need for more accommodation, staff and equipment, something that London University was still pressing for. During the war the College had continued to borrow from legacies and endowments to meet shortfalls in revenue costs, and by the end of the financial year in 1946 the General Account was £13,000 in debt.

War Veterans

Many of the new students coming in at the end of the war were ex-servicemen anxious to make up for lost time and to gain qualifications for the future. As a result, men who had been through harsh times in the past six years found themselves mingling in evening classes with youths fresh from school, a situation that sometimes caused tension. Bob McLaughlin, a naval architect studying at Paisley for his HNC just after the war, still remembers one of those classes clearly.

A native of Port-Glasgow, he moved from Lithgow's shipyard to Fleming and Ferguson's Paisley yard in order to take his HNC at Paisley Technical College. 'I stayed in digs in Old Sneddon Street during the week, and went home for the weekends. It was hard, working by day and studying in the evenings; the continual racket of tramcars passing by my window on their runs between Paisley and Renfrew and the fact that my landlord was a baker and had to get up in the early hours of the morning meant that I never got much sleep. I was always very glad to get home to Port Glasgow at the weekends!'

Because he had already gained his ONC in Port-Glasgow Mr McLaughlin was sometimes called upon to teach a class if the teacher was absent. 'In a class of about thirty, nine or ten tended to be ex-servicemen whose studies had been interrupted by the war. My heart bled for them; they were all anxious to make up for lost time, and irritated by some of the lads fresh from school, who were inclined to take the classes lightly and fool about. Once when I was teaching one particular youth became so disruptive that I finally had to order him out of the room so that those who wanted to learn could get on with it. Off he went threatening to "get his father to me," and a few evenings later, he did just that.'

Years later, recalling the moment when the irate man stormed into the classroom with his son, Bob McLaughlin admits, 'I thought my time had come. But as the lad's father advanced towards me the older ex-servicemen got up from their seats and formed a wall around me. "Don't worry, Mr McLaughlin," they said, "we'll not let him touch you." And they didn't.'

Looking back over the years, Mr McLaughlin, now retired from a full and interesting career, says, 'I could have gone to a Glasgow college, but I chose Paisley and I never regretted it. I made a lot of friends there.'

John Denholm

In 1946 the Governors finally decided to advertise the post of Principal and John Denholm, now almost 70 years of age, was free to retire. His son James took over as Acting Principal until such time as a new Principal could be appointed.

In their Minutes of June 12th 1947, the Governors recorded their gratitude for his 43-year service, and their admiration for the way in which he had 'unselfishly devoted his whole energies to the College at all times, particularly during the war years.'

They were faced with the task of finding a new Registrar as well as a new Principal, since John Denholm had filled both offices. This remarkable man, with no formal education behind him, had served the College as Registrar, teacher, Head of Physics and, finally, as acting Principal for six years during difficult and demanding circumstances.

Praise from those who knew him is unstinting. Some, like Stuart Emery, recall him as 'Smallish, and always very dapper . . . very perfect in many ways.' Claud McNeil says, 'He was a great wee chap, very systematic.'

Miss Margaret White, who worked in Gardner's law office and had dealings with the College between 1926 and 1962, recalls John Denholm as '. . . a very nice, gentle homely wee man,' and Ronald Scott, a student in the 1940s, thought him 'a dynamic sort of person.'

Dr Johnston F. Robb, another student in the early 1940s, says, 'John Denholm's particular speciality was physics, and he personally conducted evening classes in addition to his administrative duties. He was a bundle of energy, who ran everything and inspired everyone who came into contact with him. To say that he was loved by his students was no exaggeration, and I personally owe him a huge debt of gratitude.'

John Denholm played his full part in the history of the institution and when in 1980 the Rt. Hon. George Younger, then Secretary of State for Scotland, formally opened the College's Denholm Building, many people felt that at last John Denholm had been accorded the honour due to him.

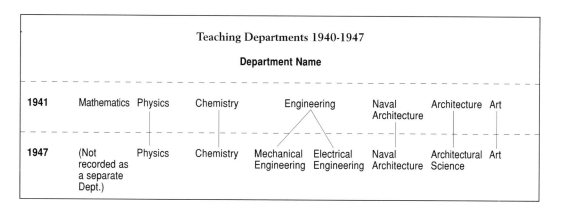

Teaching Departments 1940-1947							
Department Name							
1941	Mathematics	Physics	Chemistry	Engineering		Naval Architecture	Architecture	Art
1947	(Not recorded as a separate Dept.)	Physics	Chemistry	Mechanical Engineering	Electrical Engineering	Naval Architecture	Architectural Science	Art

Chapter 5
Principal Hugh Henry
(1947-1966)

There were forty-one applications for the post of Principal, with James Denholm and Alex McCrorie, both valued lecturers, in the short leet. When the SED cut the list to a final six names, however, they omitted both men and added the name of Hugh N. Henry, then Head of the Department of Mechanical and Electrical Engineering at Coatbridge Technical College. In April 1947 he became the new Principal of Paisley Technical College, with James Denholm as Deputy Principal.

Principal Henry.

Hugh Henry was born and raised on the Duke of Hamilton's estate, where his father worked. As boys, he and the Duke's heir shared a love of boxing. After leaving school at the age of 14 he attended evening classes while apprenticed to an engineering company in Motherwell, and in his mid-twenties he became a student at Glasgow's Royal Technical College, where he worked for two years as a research assistant in the Mechanical Engineering Department after graduating. He then joined the staff of Swindon Technical College, moving back to Scotland in 1942 to take up the post at Coatbridge Technical College. During his career he gained both industrial and academic experience.

End of an Era

Hugh Henry's appointment, together with that of Frank Phillips of Babcock & Wilcox to the Board of Governors, broke the 'Paisley pattern' set by the previous 50 years. The first two Principals had not been local men, but all Angus McLean's attention had been focused on getting the School/College onto its feet and into working order, and Lewis Richardson was more interested in his beloved research than in anything else. Until the advent of Frank Phillips, the Board of Governors had consisted mainly of local men following local tradition, wary of being overwhelmed by Glasgow institutions and therefore somewhat suspicious of any attempt to broaden the College's horizons.

Now Hugh Henry and Frank Phillips, working in tandem, blew a wind of change through the institution.

Wear and Tear

Paisley, with its variety of industries, had weathered the war years quite well, but the College itself was beginning to suffer from years of financial hardship by the time Hugh Henry became Principal. The original wiring from 1899 was still in the main George Street building, and rewiring and repairs were urgently needed both in the College buildings and in the Principal's official residence, which had had little done to it since being renovated for Principal Richardson 20 years earlier. John Earls, a full-time engineering student, recalls that in the 1940s the load-bearing capacity of the electronics laboratory was so weakened that all movement had to be restricted to the room's perimeter.

As had happened after the First World War, ex-servicemen returning to 'Civvy Street' swelled the student ranks. Ronald Scott, who had to interrupt his studies at the end of 1944 when he was called up, recalls that when he returned to the College in 1947, 'The equipment at that time was very basic but adequate. There was a steam engine and a gas engine in the Heat Engine lab, but there were still no student facilities. No refectory, no Students' Union, nothing like that. The students made significant use of Paisley Central Library's reference section, because there was no College Library. There was no social life at that time, and the classes were much bigger . . . my class was almost entirely made up of ex-service people.'

By the 1947/8 session, when there were about 2,000 enrolments, the estimated cost of essential repairs was £8,000, and a further deficit of £4,500 was forecast for the General Account, which already had a deficit of £13,000.

Return to Peace-time –
Ronald Scott and Donald Stevenson

Ronald Scott also found a new Principal in residence after the war. 'I don't think that Hugh Henry was quite the gentleman that John Denholm was,' he says. 'He was a bit more of a rough diamond.'

Donald Stevenson, no longer required by the Royal Ordnance Factory in Bishopton once the war ended, went into full-time study in the College during the mid-forties. 'There were relatively few full-time students then, only three or four in my class. Day release education had just started, and basically, we were left on our own, and expected to find things out by asking questions.'

A year after becoming a full-time student, Donald was called up and did his military service from 1946-48. He then did another year's full-time study, and after completing the BSc (Special) examination in Chemistry, he was invited, in September 1949, to join Paisley Technical College's staff. 'I came home late one Sunday night to be informed by my mother that I was to phone James Denholm, no matter when I came in. I did so, and was told that the College had a lot of students, and they wanted me to become a lecturer. He told me to come in on the following Tuesday to let him know my decision, but I didn't get the chance to accept the invitation properly. When I went in on the Tuesday, I was told that a small physics class was waiting for me to go along and teach them.'

With the expansion of day release courses, Donald was taken onto the Chemistry Department staff, where he worked under Joe McLean with Claud McNeil, Humphrey Goudie and Fred Allen. 'By then, day release was a strong element of College life. We had a lot of daywork that hadn't been there previously.'

Johnston F. Robb's part-time study at Paisley for his BSc Engineering Intermediate examinations had been brought to an abrupt halt in his second year when he was seconded from Scott's of Greenock, where he worked as a design draughtsman, to a research station on Tyneside. He completed his BSc (Eng) Final, Part I studies in England, but was appalled, when enrolling for Part II in 1947, to discover that, as he was the only mechanical engineering student requesting this course, it had been abandoned.

'I immediately contacted Jim Denholm, then Acting-Principal in Paisley (filling the gap between his father's departure and Hugh Henry's appointment) and he urged me to get my employers to release me so that I could return there to study for the Part II course on a full-time basis. If I could do that, he said, then he would try to run such a course.'

Johnston Robb's employers agreed, and in September 1947 he enrolled in Paisley, one of a class of four. 'Once again,' he says, 'I was greatly indebted to the Paisley Technical College.'

Even then life was far from smooth, for the College did not possess copies of past London University papers for the final exam. There were, however, sets of the papers in Glasgow's Mitchell Library, so the determined young student used his free Wednesday afternoons to travel to Glasgow,

Engineering Lecturers Ian Shepherd, Sandy Morton, Ken Donaldson and John Edmiston, pictured at the 1956 staff outing.

'. . . eating my two cheese rolls on the way. Over many weeks I copied out longhand some 256 final exam questions, including many drawings associated with them, and made these available to the College and the other members of the class. There was no social life for me in those days!

'Ian Shepherd, who had been appointed lecturer in the Electrical Power class, was still working out his notice in Manchester. He didn't arrive in Paisley until Christmas, and worked out his guts for us all, up to exam time in July.'

Dr Robb was impressed, too, by lecturer Alex McCrorie, recalling that on one occasion he took the trouble to travel to the Greenock home of one of his students to enquire as to how the young man's exam preparations were getting on.

In the late 1940s, when Dr Robb was completing his studies at Paisley, Alex McCrorie was past retiral age, but still Head of the Mechanical Engineering Department. 'My own speciality was thermodynamics, so I didn't need to bother him very much. Our classroom was literally a large cupboard on the top floor of the old College building, containing four desks and a blackboard. I have many recollections of tip-toeing out of the room and going for my bus, leaving Mr McCrorie fast asleep in his seat.

'The one thing that all the College lecturers shared, irrespective of their varying abilities, was their anxiety to be as helpful to us all as possible. I shall always be grateful to Paisley Technical College in general, and to the Denholms in particular, for their efforts and kindness to me in shaping my subsequent career all those years ago. I tried to repay some of my debts by becoming a Governor and serving on the Board from 1976 to 1989.'

Apprentice-Training

The apprentice-training scheme arranged between John Denholm and Frank Phillips had gone into operation, and Johnston F. Robb recalls the years 1947 and 1948 as 'the start of the great Babcock invasion . . . several double-decker buses lay outside every day at lunchtime to take the Babcock apprentices to their works canteen.'

At that time the College had no canteen and no recreational facilities, and students less fortunate than those employed by Babcock and Wilcox either brought in sandwiches to eat wherever they could, or ate at local cafes.

There was still no canteen for students in 1955 when draughtsman William Dodge, on completing his National Service, was sent to Paisley College on day-release to gain his HNC by his employers, a Kilmarnock firm of hydraulic engineers. 'I got my ONC in Kilmarnock, but they didn't cover HNC qualifications.'

Mr Dodge and his colleagues ate their lunch in a High Street cinema restaurant. 'One regular patron smoked a large cigar throughout his meal, taking a puff every few mouthfuls. Needless to say, after eating a three-course lunch plus coffee in such surroundings, we had difficulty in remaining awake during the afternoon classes.'

Letter to an Absent Graduate...

BREDILAND HOUSE,
BREDILAND ROAD,
PAISLEY.
April, 1957.

THE Hostel flourishes. We have now more residents than ever before, and our list of nation-alities is as large as ever, our latest acquisition being a young man from Colombia.

The road is now finished and has brought with it a sole advantage, a new bus route, the stop outside the hostel being greatly appreciated by the more late rising members of the hos-tel who are now able to enjoy a leisurely breakfast seated in a strategic place by the dining room window. When the bus appears in the distance they may be seen running to Brediland Road with a briefcase in one hand and a piece of toast in the other.

On the social side, since the last letter, both a Christmas Party and a Valentine Dance proved enjoyable. The success of the party, which was held at the hostel, was contributed to in no small way by the delightful female company from the RAI, and also by the efforts of Mr and Mrs Irvine, who now seem to have really settled down. Incidentally, Mr Irvine chases cows around the grounds to keep himself fit.

The dance, at the Sheiling, was somewhat hampered by the non appearance of the band. Later, however, the whole thing went with quite a swing and a good time was had by all.

The transport position in these days is rather confusing. The grounds of the hostel look extremely like a public car park, but of the nine cars only two are ever seen in motion. One of the recent acquisitions, an old Standard, focused considerable police interest on the hostel, its owner being now known by his Christian name at the police office. At the time of writing, the use of the car has been discontinued owing to its having been impounded by the police. A Funeral procession to the breakers' yard is being planned.

Yours,

MGRON

Life for Babcock students in Brediland House Paisley, as drawn and described in *GESA* in 1957.

By 1947, day release students from John Brown's and Yarrows' shipyards were also attending Paisley. Former student Claud McNeil, who became a lecturer in 1947, taught applied maths to the shipyard apprentices. The classes were large, with between 30/50 students, and difficult to deal with. 'They were having a day off work. It was hard, hard work.' Claud used football analogies to hold the students' interest.

He had applied for a lecturing post in Paisley on the suggestion of James Denholm, who wrote to tell him that they were trying to build the College up. 'As well as teaching by day, I was forced to do five nights a week,' he recalls. 'It was almost part of the conditions of employment.' In 1949 he started teaching Organic Chemistry.

Annual Outings

As well as continuing the 'family feeling' that, it is generally agreed by staff of the time, existed in the College, Hugh Henry supported the annual staff outings in late May each year. These consisted of golf in the mornings, bowling in the afternoons followed by a dinner and presentation of trophies. The entire staff attended, playing golf and bowls, even if they had never played them before. Professor John Smyth, who started teaching Biology in 1955, missed his first annual outing because of a previously-arranged

College staff pictured on the annual outing in 1955. Left to right: Joseph McLean, Alex McCrorie, Ron Williamson, Jim Denholm, Ian Shepherd and Charlie Alford (Principal Richardson's janitor and technician before the Second World War).

Fred Allan, Chemistry Lecturer whose activities were described in verse by James Jack.

"Whene'er the College held a spree
There in the midst wid Freddie be
The College Trip - the Annual Dance
Fred led them a' wi' merry prance
Mony's the madly wild Scottische
He's led us at the Cafe Riche
When no' on dance flair madly foolin'
He'd organise oor gowf an' boolin'
An' these events o' fun an' cheer
Were aye the highlights o' the year"

excursion for day-release students. 'That didn't go down at all well – you were expected to be at the staff outing.'

'Everyone, but everyone, went to the staff day out,' another lecturer recalls. The College was closed for the event and Principal Henry did not stand on his dignity on the outings, but took part alongside the rest of his staff. The outings were organised by Fred Allan of the Department of Chemistry. Generally agreed by all who knew him to be a great character,' Fred was a skilled musician and dance band leader who once a year led a 15-piece orchestra in Green's Playhouse in Glasgow.

ICI (Ardeer Division)

In 1871 Alfred Nobel, the inventor of dynamite and the man who gave his name to the Nobel Peace Prize, operated factories in Sweden, Germany, Norway and Austria, and was eager to set up another in Britain. Receiving support for his proposal in Glasgow, he began the search for a site where nitro-glycerine explosives could be manufactured, and found the perfect location at Ardeer, on the north Ayrshire coast of the Clyde estuary.

In a letter to a friend, Nobel described Ardeer as 'the most depressing place in the world . . . everlasting bleak dunes . . . only the rabbits find some nourishment, eating a substance which quite unjustifiably goes by the name of grass. It is a wonderful sand desert where the wind always blows and often howls.'

In 1926 the Nobel Explosives Company became an important section of the newly formed ICI (Imperial Chemical Industries Ltd), and in the mid to late 1940s Paisley College and the Ardeer Division developed an apprenticeship-training scheme along the same lines as that already in operation for Babcock and Wilcox. The agreement resulted in over 100 ICI apprentices and trainees attending the College on day release for ONC, HNC and degree courses in chemistry, and an ICI representative was co-opted onto the Board of Governors.

In ICI in Ayrshire, and Babcock and Wilcox in Renfrew, the College had at last found the links with local industry that it had been seeking since its inception.

The Growing Need for CI Status

Despite this success in attracting apprentices from two major companies Paisley Technical College, still without CI status, was becoming more and more isolated financially as various Acts and Reports underlined the differences between Technical Colleges like itself and the Central Institutions. A Scottish report in 1946 for example agreed in general with Lord Percy's Report of 1928, and also pointed out that Scotland was 'woefully ill-equipped' where local technical Colleges were concerned.

The Education (Scotland) Act of 1946, which obliged local education authorities to provide facilities for further education, and the Central Institutions (Scotland) Act of 1947, which relieved local authorities of the obligation of giving grant assistance to Central Institutions, put Renfrewshire Education Authority into a difficult position. Clearly, CI status was desirable for Paisley Technical College in the interests of both college and education authority.

A meeting in March 1948 between College authorities and Renfrewshire's Director of Education resulted in a fresh request from the College to the SED for Central Institution recognition, on the grounds that a) it had a long and successful record of work at degree level in science and engineering, b) that the bulk of its full-time degree-level students came from various parts of Scotland and England, and c) that in co-operation with Renfrewshire Education Authority, the College was in the process, like the Central Institutions, of shedding some of its non-advanced courses.

It also pointed out that its promotion to CI status would 'enhance the industrial prestige of the area' and 'attract support from firms of international repute.' This, in turn, would make it possible for the College to expand and to enlarge its facilities for advanced level work.

As had happened so often in Paisley's history, Glasgow's close proximity posed a threat to the outcome. The Director of Glasgow Royal Technical College opposed the application for CI status, proposing instead that Paisley should affiliate with his College and function as a centre for the lower stages of some of the Royal's diploma courses.

In the struggle for CI status, Frank Phillips, in his dual role as a member of the Board of Governors and the representative of one of the West of Scotland's main employers, gave the College strong support. So did Renfrewshire Education Authority, which was already working on its own plans to develop technical education throughout Renfrew County, including Paisley and Greenock.

As part of this plan, the non-advanced stages of the ONC were moved from the College during the 1948/49 session to the former Oakshaw Primary School, renamed Paisley Junior Technical School and later to develop into the Reid Kerr College on Renfrew Road. Staff and equipment for the classes were provided by Paisley Technical College, and funding by the Education Authority, on the understanding that in due course the Junior College would be handed over to the Authority's full management. It was essential, if this scheme was to be workable, for Paisley Technical College to become a Central Institution, relinquishing all non-advanced courses and being funded outwith the local authority.

Fortunately, Frank Phillips impressed the Under Secretary concerned with further and higher education. Another ally was James Ferguson, HM Staff Inspector for Technical Education, who felt that the Royal Technical College was not at that time large enough to absorb all of Paisley Technical College's advanced course enrolments, and that there was a case for another College in the area concentrating on advanced studies in science and engineering. Mr Ferguson emphasised the College's industrial links with Babcock and Wilcox, ICI and J & P Coats, although the latter firm, though supportive in many ways during the College's earlier years, tended to send most of its advanced trainees to technical colleges in Bolton and Manchester.

James Denholm

As Head of Physics as well as Vice-Principal, James Denholm dealt with the College's timetable and a large section of the administrative work. Several variations of the part he played in the struggle to gain Central Institution status have been woven, over the years, into College history. One is that on the day when a party of HMIs arrived to view the place, James Denholm split his classes into two, and set up a signalling system between the main building and another block. When the Inspectors had completed one section of their tour the students all changed around at Denholm's signal.

'The students thought that this was great,' said lecturer Claud McNeil. 'There was a continuous interchange of the same students between the two lecture rooms, and the Inspectors thought that the place was very busy.'

George Haig, who joined the Physics Department staff in the session 1962/63, remembers being told that on the day of the Inspectors' visit, Jim Denholm '. . . had some of the students squinting through cardboard tubes, alleged to be optical instruments of some sort. I heard that he worked wonders with cardboard, bits of string, and sealing wax to convince the Inspectors that the College could teach to the required CI standard.'

These stories have grown with time – in reality the College succeeded on its record.

Central Institution Status

In 1950, the year Frank Phillips became Chairman of the Board of Governors, a special sub-committee of the SED made a low-key recommendation in support of Paisley Technical College's application for Central Institution status.

There were many conditions. One, aimed at giving the College regional standing, demanded a major reconstruction of the governing body and the formal representation of local authorities in the West of Scotland. Industry was also to be represented, and negotiations were to continue with Renfrewshire Education Authority for the progressive transfer of much of the non-advanced work still taught at the College.

Advanced work on a full-time basis, below London University degree level, would have to be developed as a Higher National Diploma, subject to the overview of the West of Scotland Joint Committee. Any moves towards independent College diplomas were banned, and the institution's co-operation with the Royal Technical College was to continue in all appropriate circumstances. Fees were required to be levelled up in line with other Central Institutions.

These conditions were agreed upon, and in November 1950, the year of John Denholm's death, the Secretary of State for Scotland confirmed Paisley Technical College as a Central Institution.

Although the SED could not take over financial responsibility for the College until the new financial year in April 1951, they agreed to meet their share of the cost of essential repairs and to try to assist with the General Account's financial deficit. In the short-term, the College might have to continue to draw on its endowments, which would eventually be consolidated under the Endowments Scheme.

Sadly, there was a price to pay. The School of Art, which had been struggling along since Glasgow's School of Art became a CI in 1912, would have to close.

Although the College had fewer full-time students than other CIs, 903 part-time day students enrolled in the 1951/2 session, almost 5% of the total Scottish day-release enrolment at that time, and by far the largest

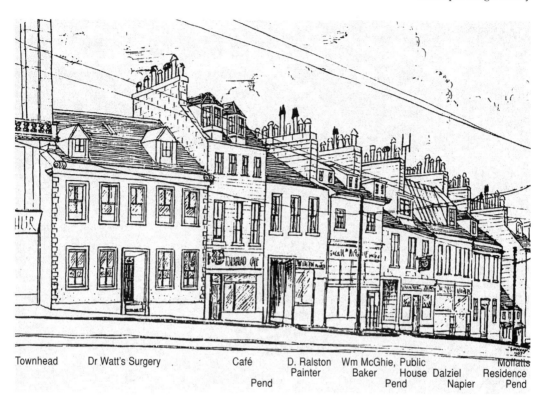

Townhead   Dr Watt's Surgery   Café   D. Ralston   Wm McGhie, Public   Moffatts
                                       Painter   Baker   House   Dalziel   Residence
                            Pend   Pend   Napier   Pend

Paisley High Street before the expansion of the College in the early 1960s. A drawing from *GESA*, May 1957.

day-release enrolment among the CIs. In view of these figures, the SED agreed in principle that there was need for a substantial extension to cope with expanding enrolments.

As a site acquired from J & P. Coats, behind the line of buildings fronting onto George Street, was not considered to be sufficient for their needs, the College authorities began negotiations with the Town Council for land at Townhead Terrace, as well as a stretch of the High Street. The discussions, involving the acquisition and demolition of old tenement property on High Street, realignment of part of the street, and alterations to the Town Council's own plans for the area, took place at both government, department and local authority levels, and lasted until 1958. At the same time the College was in discussion with the SED regarding the reappraisal of original building plans.

Evening-classes, recalls Ronald Scott, who returned to the College as a part-time lecturer in 1951, were 'very much what the College depended on in those days. Most, if not all, the part-time staff were evening lecturers. There existed an informal system of arranging lecturers in the evenings. . . . I don't even remember if they asked if I knew what the hell I was talking about!' After graduating from Paisley College Mr Scott had taken up a post at ICI's Research Station at Ardeer – 'In those days it wasn't a case of wondering whether I would get a job, but rather which job I would take. I could have gone to any one of a number of companies.'

The School of Art

In 1953, the School of Art which had originally developed from the Government School of Design in Gilmour Street, closed down. Its equipment was handed over to Renfrewshire Education Authority for use in schools, and a number of casts were sent to Glasgow School of Art. The premises vacated by the School of Art were converted to Physics laboratories.

As well as the architect Thomas Tait, other well-known names passed through Paisley Art Department. Bill Gallacher, nephew of MP Willie Gallacher, spent a year in Paisley before moving to Glasgow School of Art. His father, a trades union official, painted union banners on silk. Paisley-born Alexander Adams, on the staff of Paisley's Art Department in the 1920s, went on to become Head of the Architecture Department at Glasgow School of Art, and Graham Henderson, Head of Building Construction at Paisley in the early 1920s, later became the first Scottish President of RIBA (Royal Institute of British Architects).

Hugh Adam Crawford, an evening lecturer, became Principal of Duncan of Jordanstone College of Art, now part of Dundee University, where a building bears his name. Paisley artist Alexander MacPherson, who taught in the College in the 1930s, was principal art teacher at John Neilson High School for 25 years. He died in 1970, and in 1996 a number of his paintings raised over £14,000 when sold at auction.

David R. Dunn

In 1905, David R. Dunn had become a student-teacher in the Art Department, going on to devote his entire working life to the institution, apart from an absence during the First World War when he held a commission as a squadron leader in the Royal Flying Corps.

His daughter, Mrs Meg Ferguson, recalls being told of a meeting he had in the skies with the famous German pilot, the Red Baron. 'The Red Baron, being a gentleman, signalled that he was going to shoot my father down.' Sensibly, David Dunn turned his aircraft homewards and survived to return to Paisley.

He took his Art Diploma in Glasgow in 1921 and eventually became Head of Paisley College's Art Department. His paintings were frequently exhibited, and he was also interested in leatherwork, brass, and china and wood painting. Mrs Ferguson remembers that her father was worried at times about the Art School's future, probably because of its close proximity to the Glasgow School of Art.

Mrs McDougall, whose sister Tina Wilkie was one of David Dunn's students in the twenties and thirties, says, 'Mr Dunn was a very kind man, and so helpful. Tina had a happy association with the Tech and made a lot of friends there.'

David Dunn was with the College for half a century, probably the longest personal association in its history. He worked closely with local schools and was responsible for setting up the town's Junior School of Art. After

David Dunn pictured in the Art
Department, G Block.

retiring in 1953 he continued to enjoy an active life right up until his
death in 1976, aged 88 years. He ranks among those who have left their
imprint on the University of Paisley for all time.

Finances and Links with Paisley

The Paisley Technical College Scheme 1954, set up to deal with the
overall running of the College as a CI, required the institution to
consolidate its endowments. These totalled approximately £36,000, of
which more than £17,000 was owed by the General Account. The SED
allowed the College to borrow and then repay a loan from its revenue
to meet this debt, and permitted a similar device to enable it to meet
its 40% share of capital expenditure under the funding arrangements
which applied until 1959.

Although funding was now provided by central government, the links
with the town of Paisley were retained through the presence, on the Board
of Governors, of the Provost and a reduced representation from the Brough
Trustees.

Students' Representative Council

By now the students were beginning to organise their own affairs, both
administrative and social. A Students' Representative Council was
established and affiliated to the Scottish Union of Students, and there were
monthly dances, snooker and billiards competitions as well as an Annual

Paisley Tech. News

SPRING has arrived. To the "layman" this statement is apt to conjure up various seasonal fantasies such as young animals unsteady on their feet aping the antics of their fond parents, various shades of greenery carpeting the land, flower buds enticed out to meet the new warmth of the sun and the heralds of Spring busying themselves in the full-throated industry of home building. To the student of Paisley Technical College these typical scenes of Spring are apparent, but unfortunately not fully appreciated, because for him there is an additional seasonable aspect to be considered, one upon which no bard has thought to romance; I mean examinations. Thus the general atmosphere in 28 George Street is rather depressing, brightened only by weekly visits to Renfrew and chance views, through an open hatch, of what "makes the typewriters tick." From all reports the degree classes are preparing themselves well for the forthcoming examination—Bless them. As for G.C.E. members—well!—they might as well have my blessing too, for I cannot at present name anyone else who will give them their's.

"All work and no play makes Jack a dull boy" is the maxim that has been revered to the extent of one Saturday each month being given over to College Dances. These dances have been a great success as the S.R.C. funds—We hope—will show. The bands hired could not quite be described as orchestras, neither could they be condemned as Rock and Roll outfits, but rather a happy medium whose rhythm compelled one's foot to sympathise with the drum beat, often on top of someone else's foot; but the hall never was very large.

A description of a College dance c. 1957 from *GESA*.

Ball. A lack of evening accommodation curtailed the students' social life somewhat but, as an article of the time in the Babcock and Wilcox student newsletter *Gesa*, says, perhaps that was just as well as far as exam results were concerned.

Gordon Macaulay, a student from 1950 to 1954, and a staff member in the Mechanical Engineering Department from 1957-1990, describes those monthly 'Saturday night hops' in the Gardner Hall in G Block as 'warm and sweaty affairs.' During one of them an inebriated student wrote rude slogans on the board of one of the lecture rooms – in English, Latin, Greek and French. 'Educated graffitti,' comments Mr McAuley. It is understood that the student in question was gently carpeted on the following Monday morning.

The Biology Department

The first-year course for the Pharmaceutical Chemists' certificate, set up in 1955 through an arrangement with the Royal Technical College, brought Biology into the College curriculum on a full-time basis, and led to the appointment of John C. Smyth (later to become Professor Smyth) who had been an assistant lecturer in Edinburgh University's Department of Zoology.

Professor Smyth's interview for the post was 'more of a pleasant chat with Principal Henry, James Denholm and Joseph McLean, at the end of which I discovered that I had the job without really trying, as it were.'

His first impressions on taking up his new post were of 'extreme informality' and 'a bit of a culture shock.' He did, however, find that people were 'extremely friendly and anxious to help. At first, Biology was part of the Chemistry Department, with the use of a laboratory on the top floor of G Block. There wasn't really any equipment at all and I could not believe

Professor John C Smyth.

in the informality in ordering some. We put up a biology library in our main staff-room.'

Any hopes the College might have nurtured that the Royal Technical College would eventually pass on its entire Pharmaceutical certificate course were soon dashed. The Royal was in fact planning to phase the course out entirely, and once this was realised Paisley took steps to shed it. The other course running at the time was the endorsed certificate of the Institute of Biology, later to become a National Certificate course. Its first students were technicians from the University of Glasgow, but later the class expanded to take in technicians from other universities and research institutes, attending the College for one day and one evening a week.

In time the new department 'spread in G Block like a cancerous growth, in the view of some of the other departments,' says Professor Smyth. More accommodation was required and for a while it was thought that the small Biology staff-room could be used to house the Department's animals. As the accommodation of animals in such institutions is governed by Home Office regulations, a Home Office Inspector was called in to consider the suggestion. It was dropped when the Inspector put his head round the staff-room door, took one look, and told the staff members present, 'This room is quite unsuitable for animals!'

During the early 1960s, the Biology Department was blamed for a mouse epidemic in G Block; in fact, says Professor Smyth, the problem was quite the reverse – a male wild mouse had managed to squeeze through the bars of the cage holding the Biology mice, and as a result some curiously-coloured babies were born. 'I did once see one of our cockroaches crawling over the ceiling above the stairs,' Professor Smyth admits, 'but we didn't talk too much about that.'

One of his favourite stories, stemming from general nervousness over the inhabitants of the Department's animal room, concerns a new baby brought in on a visit by its proud parent, a former student. As the child's cries filtered through the building an engineer remarked, 'I knew these biologists would overdo it sometime!'

By 1958 the department was teaching the first-year higher endorsed certificate course and had also started the London GCE A-level, mainly for students, some of them from abroad, who were trying to upgrade their school qualifications to equip them for courses such as medicine. The course later developed into London degree work in Biology.

Staff Interviews

Like Professor Smyth, Gordon Macaulay had also experienced a casual interview when, in 1957, he returned to the College as a staff member 'almost by mistake,' after doing his National Service in the RAF. Due to a shortage of staff in Paisley at that time, he was asked by John Edmiston if he would be interested in taking up a lecturer's post. 'There was no interview as such, just a ten-minute meeting with Principal Hugh Henry, who gave me five good general reasons why I shouldn't go into the teaching profession.' This, Mr McAuley feels on looking back over the years, may have been the Principal's way of advising him to beware of what he was getting himself into.

In Mr Macaulay's case, he was getting himself into marriage; he and Yvonne Carmichael of the Biology Department announced their engagement at one of the annual staff outings, and their wedding in 1963 was 'very much a College event.'

Successful Students

When Eddie Mullen began working at Ardeer as a laboratory assistant, 'day release at "the Tech" in Paisley was a condition of employment for ICI's trainee laboratory assistants. Everyone went there.' ICI's standards were high; their students were required to take their ONC in two years, followed by a further two years' study for their HNC, with 60% passes in all subjects. Any student failing to achieve the required minimum had to repeat his or her studies at evening class in the following year. On gaining the HNC, the students were then expected to go on to complete the Certificate of Paisley College, which was a passport into the 3rd year of a 4-year Honours course at Glasgow's Royal College of Science and Technology (now Strathclyde University).

A.D. Mitchell and D.A. Paterson in a Chemistry lab in the Bow Wing c. 1955.

'Paisley was away ahead of the game in the fifties,' says Eddie, who recalls the College at that time as being 'a bit run down . . . the lab had solid wooden benches and not a lot of equipment; it was all test-tube stuff, no instruments in those days.' ICI donated a lot of laboratory equipment to Paisley.

After work experience, which took him all over the world and eventually led to the position of a senior plant manager at Ardeer, Eddie became Safety Officer at Paisley College in February 1991.

The combination of ICI's high standards and the College's teaching system led to great things for many ICI students. One of Eddie Mullen's student associates, Jack Smith, later emigrated to America, where he eventually became Vice President of Ensign Bickford, an American explosives company. Eddie recalls reading in the Nobel Times, ICI's newsletter, that on Jack Smith's appointment to the post, Ensign Bickford made a grant to Paisley Technical College.

Another ICI student, William J. Rodger, became Head of Strathclyde Police Forensic Department. The oldest of a family of five, he was anxious to continue his education, and was delighted to be sent on day-release to Paisley after obtaining a job at Ardeer.

He, too, thought that the College's laboratories were very basic, used as he was to ICI's operational and analytical laboratories. 'It was a bit run-down by comparison to ICI . . . dreary, dull, dismally decorated, if it was decorated at all. But the opportunity for me was tremendous, and I was able to continue my studies. Day release was a break, in a way, from the demands of the job – a very enjoyable day. Paisley Tech did an excellent job at the time – I don't think there is any doubt about that. There was a good rapport, with no "them and us" scenario. We were all part of the game.' Professor Rodger went on to study in Glasgow's Royal College, and after leaving ICI to take a PhD at Glasgow University via the Royal College, he started work with Glasgow Police.

The College in the 1950s and early '60s

In April 1950, a dinner was held to mark the College's Jubilee, a date again taken from 1900, when the Duke of Argyll formally opened the original George Street building. Sheriff Hamilton, Chairman of the Governors for the previous ten years, was in attendance, as was former Principal Lewis Fry Richardson. Mr Ian P. Coats, a member of the textile family that had been so closely involved from the College's earliest days, proposed the toast. A Jubilee students' dance was held in Paisley Town Hall.

A ticket for the College Jubilee Dinner.

Paisley Technical College and School of Art

Jubilee Dinner Ticket

(Gibsons' Rooms, 20th April, 1950, at 7 p.m.)

No....35. *One Guinea paid.*

During the 1950s, Pressed Steel took over Beardmore's former munitions plant in Linwood, close by Paisley, and started making railway wagons and carriage frames. By 1955 they were employing 2,000 people, a number matched by the Rolls Royce factory at Hillington Industrial Estate. But unfortunately for

John Anderson, a student at Paisley (University of London BSc Hons 1950) pictured here as a lecturer in Mechanical Engineering between 1950 and 1954. He returned as Head of Department in 1958. While he was Head the Department developed HND, CNAA Ordinary, Honours and Postgraduate degrees and was involved in many consultancy and research projects.

Wallace Redpath, Mechanical Engineering lecturer pictured in 'G' Block in 1954.

A class of Mechanical Engineers photographed in Room 27, 'G' Block in 1954. Left to right: Peter Reynolds, Alex Mckenzie, Joseph Kerr, Gordon Macaulay, Ian Scarlett, Ian Macaulay, Geoffrey Spencer, David Burgess, Alan Clark, Jimmy Simpson and Peter Barker.

Equipment in the
Mechanical
Engineering
laboratory
(situated in the old
Barbour/Dyeworks
Wing now
demolished)
including materials
testing machinery
and steam engine,
c. 1960.

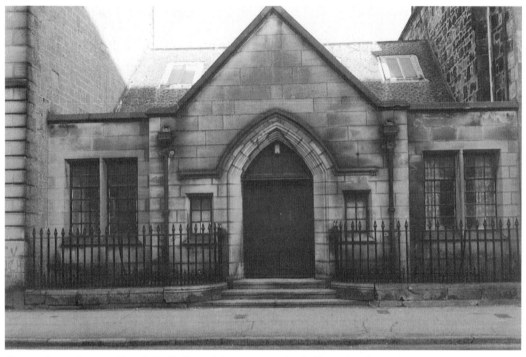

George Street Baptist Church Hall. One of the many Paisley halls used as lecture rooms during this period.

Westerfield House, High Calside, Paisley purchased by the College in 1955.

College office staff c. 1960. Left to right: Margaret Casey, Eleanor Jones and Marion Campbell.

Rita Wilson, Chemistry technician, c. 1960.

Norma Shand, and Elizabeth Lawrie, Physics Department technicians, c. 1960.

Paisley Technical College, neither of the two large companies was committed to working in conjunction with local technical education.

As new industry moved in, however, the older industries weakened, and by the end of the decade, two of Paisley's major dye-works had closed, as had Dobie's tobacco factory.

The College was still growing in size and in stature. In 1953/54, all four of the successful Scottish candidates in the Associateship of the Royal Institute of Chemistry examination came from Paisley, and in the 1954/55 session the first two students presented from Paisley for the Institute of Physics graduation examinations passed. In 1955/56, the first session in which the College presented candidates for the Intermediate examination of the Pharmaceutical Society of Great Britain, it achieved a 100% result.

Accommodation was a major problem. Much of the textile work had been moved to rooms made available by J & P. Coats at Ferguslie, and in 1955 the College bought Westerfield, a substantial Victorian house at Calside, with two cottages in its grounds, for classroom purposes. Local church halls were leased, and temporary huts erected on the sites awaiting expansion.

The administrative staff was still very small. Margaret MacNab, the Principal's secretary, was in charge of the office and its staff, consisting of Isabel Hart and Jenny Urquhart. All College admissions were handled by the General Office, with the staff writing up the registers and the record-cards by hand. The 'family' atmosphere had endured, despite the change to CI status, and during Principal Henry's time the lecturers and many full-time students were on first-name terms.

Marion Campbell, who joined the administrative staff in 1955, will never forget her job interview. Fifteen years of age and fresh from Paisley South School's classrooms, Marion was met on her arrival at the College by 'a tall handsome gentleman dressed smartly in a navy suit, white shirt and black tie,' who proceeded to cross-examine her.

'Can you type?' he wanted to know. 'Do you have shorthand, and can you make a good cup of tea?' Marion, doing her best to answer the questions to his satisfaction, later discovered that he was John Allison, the head janitor, and that her 'real' interview, with the Principal, was still to come.

John Allison, janitor photographed in 1956.

Professor William McEwan of the Quality Centre, a student at the College in 1951/52, recalls John Allison clearly. 'He had a stature like one of the Coldstream Guards. No-one stepped out of line with him.'

At that time most of the College technicians and janitors tended to be ex-Royal Navy personnel, and many of the non-academic female staff were widows. There also tended to be a family connection among non-academic staff, with sisters, brothers, parents, sons and daughters following what had become family tradition.

Building Plans

In 1957, Paisley Technical College launched a £200,000 appeal, aimed at industry, commerce, and other local interests, for funds to build the proposed new extension. Although Babcock & Wilcox and the Nobel Division of ICI supported the fund – Babcock donated £50,000 and ICI donated £15,000 'in . . . commendation of the training and teaching given at Paisley Technical College,' the Governors were disappointed by the amount yielded by small individual contributions. When the appeal closed, about £155,000 had been gathered in.

An architectural competition to find the best design for the extension resulted in the submission of over 500 designs, with first place going to the Edinburgh firm of Alison, Hutcheson & Partners. A model of their design went on show in the College, together with designs from the runners-up.

In 1958, the college acquired the land it needed from the Town Council. It was agreed that funding for the major extension would be met in part by the College on a 40/60 formula out of an original total estimated cost of £500,000.

Course Development

Also in 1958 the Board of Governors set up a Policy Committee to consider the College's general development, partly in answer to general staff unease over the future, caused by the decanting of non-advanced work to the local authorities.

It was suggested that an associateship recognised by the professional institutions should be set up, possibly integrated with that of the Royal Technical College (now renamed the Royal College of Science and Technology, and eventually to become Strathclyde University). Other CIs had similar associateships, but the old fear of being taken over by Glasgow made many uneasy about such a move. Nor was the Royal College itself enthusiastic.

In 1956 a White Paper on technical education in Scotland, while praising the Central Institutions for the zeal and energy of their governing bodies and their close links with the education authorities and industry, pointed out that Scotland had only 25,000 day-release students compared to around 375,000 students in England and Wales.

In response, the National Council for Technological Awards (NCTA) introduced the Diploma of Technology (DipTech) into Scotland. DipTech, which had been in operation in England and Wales for a year, was seen as a degree equivalent though without the status and title. Courses for the new award were to be mainly, but not exclusively, the province of a group of Colleges to be developed outwith Scotland as Colleges of Advanced Technology. Scotland's advanced technological colleges continued to be known as Central Institutions.

Paisley had considered adopting DipTech when it was first introduced into Scotland, but the SED had not encouraged the idea, feeling that the importation of an English-based award might devalue existing awards. Now the chief officer of NCTA, on a visit to Paisley, expressed his view that the

College might well achieve recognition as a centre for the new DipTech award on completion of the proposed extension.

Sandwich courses, so-called because they consist of alternate layers of full-time study and organised work experience, were first introduced into the College in the 1960/61 session, within the Mechanical and Civil Engineering Departments.

The Annual Report for session 1958/59 states that 'considerable thought had been given to the provision of sandwich courses that might be offered,' and continues, 'one of the main factors leading to the decision has been the change in regulations for admission to the engineering institutions. The effect of those changes is that although the route to membership of that professional engineering institutions by part time courses is not closed, it has become increasingly difficult.'

Despite these early doubts, sandwich courses, in which students combine work and study, spending periods of their course in the College and periods on placement in an industrial firm, became popular, and have revolutionised methods of study.

STECC

In 1959, the five Regional Advisory Councils set up by the SED in 1949 were replaced by the Scottish Technical Education Consultative Council (STECC), a national body. The Education Act (Scotland) Fund was also discontinued, and under new 1959 regulations Central Institutions were required to submit estimates of expenditure for the SED's approval. The grant was then restricted to the approved amount, with any additional costs being met by savings elsewhere within the budget.

The separate Maintenance and Capital Grants were combined, with a single recurrent grant to cover small capital costs of less than £5,000. Capital items needed in excess of this were to be met on their merits by a non-recurrent grant.

Students' Association and Accommodation

In Paisley, a Students' Association was formed, with an approved constitution, in 1959, and by the early 1960s an area had been set aside at Westerfield, the villa owned by the College, as a study, library and coffee bar for students.

A substantial legacy from the estate of Dr William Watt, a long-serving Governor, first elected in 1935 as a representative of Paisley Philosophical Institution, enabled the College to start acquiring flats in Townhead Terrace, close to the campus. When completed, they became the Watt Residence. Just after they had been bought, however, lecture accommodation within the College was so tight that some of the flats awaiting development had to be pressed into use. George Haig, who started teaching in the Physics Department in the early sixties, remembers taking a class of three in Townhead Terrace, in 'what had obviously been a bedroom, with a tiny blackboard and a few chairs.'

The Watt Residence is named after Dr William J C Watt a Paisley doctor who had been a student at the College before he took up medicine. He was a Governor from 1935 until 1960 when he became Chairman of the Board. He bequeathed flats in Townhead Terrace to the College which, with additional purchased flats became the Watt Residence in 1966-68.

Frank Phillips OBE

In 1959, Frank J. Phillips retired from Babcock and Wilcox, and in 1960 he retired as Chairman of the Board of Governors. Since his appointment as Education Officer with Babcock in 1945, he had worked tirelessly to obtain the best training facilities possible for the company's employees, and had been an active supporter of the College. He died in 1965, aged 70 years.

Turn-around

Arthur Hughes. Technician 1957-1987.

Work on the new extension began in 1960. The most ambitious expansion to date, it involved virtually turning the College around in a half-circle so that its new entrance fronted the High Street instead of George Street.

Arthur Hughes, a College technician between 1957 and 1987, recalls that, 'When the old Gorbals tenements in Glasgow were pulled down, the stone was seen to be excellent. The head man of the construction firm at Paisley bought the stone for his company, and it was used in the foundations of what is now A Block.'

The expansion included the removal of the old dye-works, part of the original site. This must have been good news for one lecturer, who recently recalled one of the perils of teaching in the converted dye-works. Channels originally cut into the floor to hold the dyes had worked just as well with draughts, and he had given many a lecture with the bottoms of his trousers fastened by bicycle clips, in an attempt to avert the chilly winds whistling along the deep channels. Ken Donaldson, who

A, B & D Blocks in the mid 60s. The remains of the Bow Wing known as L Block can be seen on the right of the photograph.

taught Electrical Engineering classes in the old dye-works says that they would have been closed down if they were used today. 'Cables hung from the ceilings, equipment had to be supported by wedges because of the sloping concrete floors and the distribution box had exposed brass connections. When a research student was killed at Heriot Watt, Ian Shepherd, the Head of Department, himself bought heavy rubber mats for the lab the next day.'

Break with Tradition

From the College's first days, members of the Gardner family, who owned a well-respected legal firm in Paisley, had acted as its Clerk and Treasurer, but in 1961 the 66 years-old association came to an end when James Gardner fell ill

Kenneth Caldwell, appointed Assistant Secretary from 1957, took over from Mr Gardner, and the College books, hitherto kept in the Gardner offices, were transferred to the College buildings. Miss Margaret White, who had worked for Gardners' since 1926, and whose duties had included writing the notes taken at College meetings, described the change in arrangements as, '. . . like having an arm and a leg cut off.' In 1961 most of Gardner's legal work was taken over by another Paisley law firm with whom Miss White worked for another twenty years. Sadly, James Gardner died in 1962.

The College Library

Until 1963, each department was responsible for its own library. Technician Arthur Hughes recalls that his evening duties could involve three separate tasks – Electrical Engineering technician, Mechanical Engineering technician, or Librarian. 'In those days we did everything and made everything ourselves.'

When Hamish Maclachlan became College Librarian in 1963, it took him about a year to gather, catalogue and classify the 6,000 books scattered throughout the buildings, including a distinguished collection of scientific and technical works in the main European languages, donated by James Coats Jr. in 1901. In the small room he shared in the Gardner Building with two mechanical engineering lecturers Mr Maclachlan classified and catalogued the books, then sent them back to the appropriate departments.

Early in 1965, a large ground-floor room was set up as a library. Three assistants were appointed, and the books recalled, labelled, stamped and shelved. The library opened its doors to students in October 1965.

Hamish Maclachlan, first College Librarian.

The original College Library on the mezzanine floor of the Gardner Hall in 'G' Block.

Toothill Report/Industrial Liaison Centres

By the early 1960s, there was a marked local decline in traditional heavy industries. At about this time, J & P Coats closed its huge Ferguslie Mills and merged with the English firm of Paton and Baldwin; Paisley's last shipyard, Fleming & Ferguson, also closed during the 1960s.

The Toothill Report of 1961 urged comprehensive re-development, particularly in science-based industries, and an accompanying infrastructure to support desirable industrial change. Under the Robbins Report, technical colleges in England and Wales were designated polytechnics. This was not applicable under Scottish Education Committee ruling, but the Paisley, Robert Gordon Institute, and Dundee Colleges of Technology, were considered to be comparable to the new polytechnics.

In 1963 it was decided that under the administrative co-ordination of the Department of Scientific and Industrial Research (DSIR), the Scottish technological CIs at Paisley, Aberdeen, Dundee and Edinburgh should each have Industrial Liaison Centres, run by Industrial Liaison Officers (ILOs) with the remit to develop closer liaison with local industry and to keep small manufacturing firms abreast of relevant research documentation. Such a system was already in operation in Glasgow's Royal College of Science and Technology.

John Oswald MBE

Paisley's first ILO was John Oswald, chief metallurgist at the Pressed Steel factory in Linwood, and an evening lecturer in the Chemistry Department during the 1950s.

John Oswald
MBE.

'I used to go in straight from work, with my fish supper under my arm. I had a great class – it was a lecture and lab, and sometimes, if I had been too busy at Pressed Steel to plan out my evening lecture, I set up a laboratory experiment for the class. While they were working on that I wrote my lecture.'

John Oswald's area of responsibility as an Industrial Liaison Officer covered the former south western counties of Renfrew, Ayr, Wigtown, Kirkcudbright and Dumfries, as far as the Borders. He was strongly supported in his new position by Principal Henry, who had always encouraged his staff to become involved in local industry.

'I got off the ground more quickly than my fellow ILOs because I already had local contacts and I had more support from Paisley than the other ILOs got from their colleges. I was more or less turned loose. Every six weeks I met with Principal Henry to discuss results, and I could also speak to him whenever I needed to.'

During his first year as ILO, John Oswald paid at least six visits a week to businesses in his area. 'At first I wrote to tell them that I was available, but often there was no reply, so I changed my tactics, informing them that I would call at a certain time, then turning up whether I had heard from them or not. I also made a point of dealing with executives, because they were less likely than other employees to leave the firm.'

'The original idea was that industrial problems could be referred to the DSIR research centres, but I soon realised that the College itself could solve a lot of the problems that came up. By then it was almost obligatory in the College that lecturers had to come from industry whenever possible. We began to introduce a system whereby firms got one problem solved for free, then after that they paid for the assistance they received. Some of the lecturers resented being drawn into helping industry as well as doing their own jobs – one even objected, at the beginning, to me having my coffee in the staff-room because I wasn't a lecturer – but in general I had tremendous support throughout.'

In this way, John Oswald strengthened the link between the College and local industry, knitting them into a working relationship mutual to both sides. At the same time he finally put into practice the ideas expressed in 1892 by Sheriff Cowan and in 1910 by chemistry teacher George Gardiner, thus vindicating both men.

New College Buildings Opened

By October 1963 the new buildings were finished, incorporating among other things a much-needed refectory, a common-room, library study room, and games room for students, as well as an office for the Student

The College Buildings: 1960s Expansion.

CI status, expanding student numbers and negotiations with Paisley Town Council 1953-58 resulted in the range of buildings, facing the High Street, which were formally opened in 1963. 'A', 'B' and 'D' Blocks were joined in the late 60s by 'K' Block (1968) and the Watt Residence (1966-68). Continued growth of student numbers meant that many local church halls were used as lecture rooms. The plan shows the extent of College property in 1963. Alison & Hutchison and Partners were the architects for 'A', 'B', 'C' and 'D' blocks. Macpherson and Gibson designed 'K' Block.

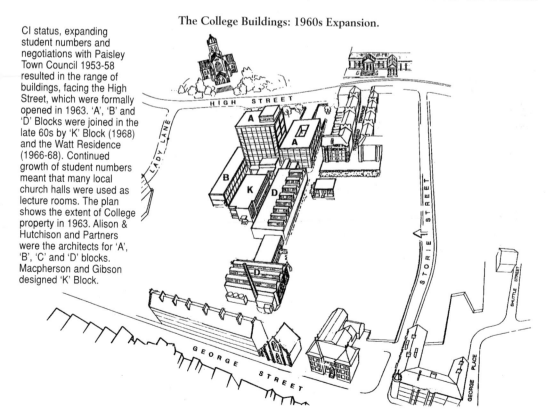

99

The new High
Street frontage,
1963. The
Barbour Tower
('A' Block) with
the Brough
Building
(including the
Brough Hall) to
the left of the
main entrance.

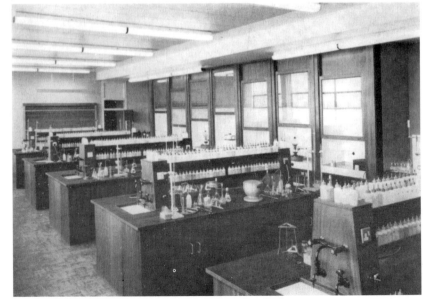

A laboratory in
the Department
of Chemistry in
'A' Block in 1963.

Biology students
c. 1963.

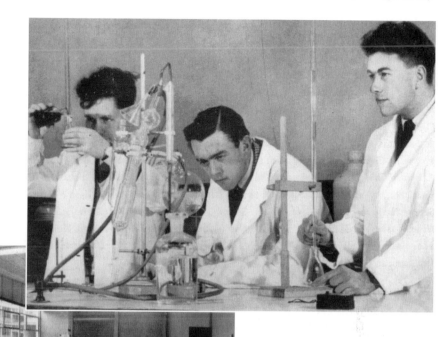

Drawing office c. 1963

Civil Engineering
Lecturers Sam
Leith and Alan
Clark testing a
concrete unit in
the Structures
Laboratory
c. 1965.

Part of the Department of Mechanical and Production Engineering in 'D' Block in 1963.

A room in the Department of Mathematics and Physics in 'B' Block in 1963.

Soil Mechanics. A laboratory in the Department of Civil Engineering and Building in 1963.

A laboratory in the Department of Electrical Engineering in 'D' Block in the early 1960s.

Representative Council (SRC) . In effect the College had done an 'about face', and now fronted onto High Street, with George Street to the rear. On October 25th 1963, the extension was formally opened by the Duke of Hamilton, a boyhood friend of Principal Henry. At the same time the College changed its name to Paisley College of Technology, though it continued to be known fondly by Paisley people as 'The Tech' – and still is in some quarters.

Academic Developments

Following the Robbins Report, the College authorities had to decide on the methods of degree-awarding powers needed to secure its academic standing, as well as finding out how to achieve expansion at a time when the science and technology classes in universities had empty seats. The 1950s and early 60s had seen a considerable development in certificate, diploma and professional courses.

In 1964, thanks to part-time courses that had started in the early 60s in Works and Supervisory Management, Paisley College of Technology was recognised as an approved centre by the National Examination Board for Supervisory Studies (NEBSS).

In the same year, Principal Henry became Chairman of the Scottish Association for National Certificates and Diplomas (SANCAD), set up to replace the old West of Scotland, South-east and North-east Joint Committees. He was also active in the Association of Principals of Technical Institutions, being Chairman of the Scottish branch for a number of years. The College's academic staff were encouraged to attend conferences and training courses and to become professionally involved with committees such as those which administered the National Certificates and Diplomas.

As the Royal College of Science and Technology, which became Strathclyde University, withdrew from National Certificate and Diploma work, Paisley College staff members became catalysts in the development of these courses. The introduction of National Certificate courses in Applied Physics, Mathematics, Chemical Engineering and Biology were the direct result of staff initiatives.

HND courses in Mechanical and Electrical Engineering and an equivalent College Diploma in Civil Engineering were introduced in the 1960/61 session, and part-time courses in Works and Supervisory Management led in 1964 to the College's recognition as an approved centre.

HND courses in Mechanical and Electrical Engineering and an equivalent Diploma in Civil Engineering were introduced in the 1960/61 session.

The Civil Engineering Department, which came to generate the highest demand for sandwich courses, set up an Industrial Training Advisory Board involving the College, employers (both local authority and construction industry) and consultants to advise on sandwich training for civil engineering and building students.

The College soon initiated its Engineering Colloquia, which enabled

EXTRACT of MATRICULATION of the A

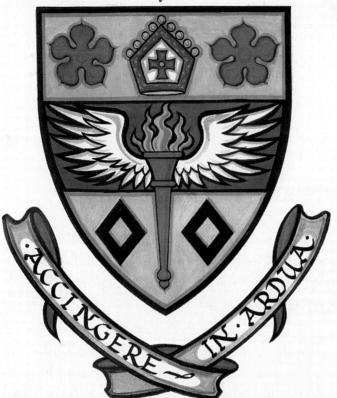

The Governors of PAISL
having by Petition unto th
were recorded of date Sev
College in the Public Regi
narrated "THAT Paisl
died on 18th July 1883,
further assisted by the do
Paisley; THAT the found
year 1895 and the transf
instruction of Students in
and adults in accordance
draft Scheme for the Colle
being approved by Her M
provisions of the Scheme,
THAT the said College w
Modelling, Design for A
able to Industries and A
and otherwise as the Gov

Scottish Education Department the title of the College as from 1 June 1963
prayed that the said Arms might be recorded of new in the said Public
Lyon King of Arms by Interlocutor of date 1 June 1963 Granted Warra
Bearings in Scotland in name of the Governors of Paisley College of Tech
between an abbots mitre proper embellished of the First accompanied by t
Third, winged Argent and enflamed of the First surmounting the fess an
Matriculated the 7th day of October 1963.
Extracted furth of the 87th page of the 45th Volume of the Public Regist
of All Arms and Bearings in Scotland this 7th day of October 1963. —

Extract of the Matriculation of the Arms of Paisley College of Technology, granted in 1963.

PAISLEY COLLEGE of TECHNOLOGY.

EGE of TECHNOLOGY, at George Street, Paisley in the County of Renfrew
on King of Arms of date 1 June 1963 Shewn :— THAT Ensigns Armorial
day of February 1954 in favour of the Governors of Paisley Technical ——
ll Arms and Bearings in Scotland (Vol. 39, fol. 143) wherein it is——
cal College was founded by the Trustees of the late Peter Brough, who—
ds accumulated by them for the purpose; THAT the foundation was—
a site, and later on of £3000 from the firm of Messrs J. and P. Coats, —
further assisted by the dissolution of the Paisley School of Design in the
ssets to the Paisley Technical College; THAT the College opened for the
on 1897-1898 and has since then carried out the instruction of children
Constitution; THAT the Secretary of State for Scotland has prepared a
Part 6 of the Education (Scotland) Act 1946, and on the draft Scheme
Council, the said Deed of Constitution, so far as inconsistent with the
e operation of Section 125 of the Act, be repealed and abrogated". —
blished for the instruction of Children and Adults in Drawing, Painting,
re, Manufactures and Decoration in Pure and Natural Sciences applic-
ures and such other subjects in Science, Art and Technical Education
ay think necessary". THAT with the approval and consent of the—
led to Paisley College of Technology; AND the Petitioners having—
in name of the Governors of Paisley College of Technology, The Lord —
Cyon Clerk to matriculate in the Public Register of All Arms and—
e following Ensigns Armorial, videlicet :— Or, a fess Azure —
foils Gules in chief, and in base two mascles Sable, a torch of the—
and in an Escrol this Motto ACCINGERE · IN · ARDUA. —

H. A. B. Lawson.

Rothesay Herald.

Lyon Clerk Keeper of the Records.

senior executives from major local industries to meet with staff and students for informal exploration of live issues in engineering, and the catchment was widened to include the National Engineering Laboratory, the Royal Radar Establishment, and the south-based research and development units of firms such as the Rootes car factory, which had by then taken over from Pressed Steel in Linwood.

Like its predecessor, Rootes did not support local technical education, and the College therefore derived little benefit from its presence, although Rootes was a local employer of major importance.

From London External to CNAA

The academic changes of the early '60s highlighted a growing problem. From the introduction of courses in 1903 and recognition as a centre in 1904 the London University's external BSc degree had been essential to the College, and an invaluable asset in the bid for CI status. But throughout the 1950s and into the 1960s there had been growing dissatisfaction with the limitations of working to a syllabus set outwith the College.

Lecturer Gordon Macaulay was aware, even during his time as a student in the 1950s, of 'an unhappiness with the London University degree courses. The staff didn't set the examinations, or mark the papers. For them, it was a rather remote affair.'

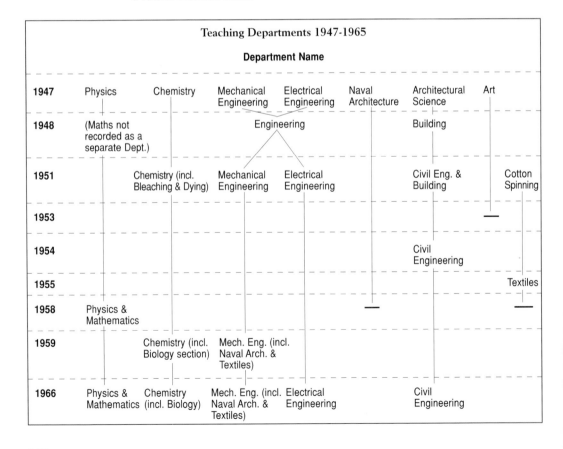

Teaching Departments 1947-1965

Department Name

Year							
1947	Physics	Chemistry	Mechanical Engineering	Electrical Engineering	Naval Architecture	Architectural Science	Art
1948	(Maths not recorded as a separate Dept.)		Engineering			Building	
1951		Chemistry (incl. Bleaching & Dying)	Mechanical Engineering	Electrical Engineering		Civil Eng. & Building	Cotton Spinning
1953							—
1954						Civil Engineering	
1955							Textiles
1958	Physics & Mathematics			—			—
1959		Chemistry (incl. Biology section)	Mech. Eng. (incl. Naval Arch. & Textiles)				
1966	Physics & Mathematics	Chemistry (incl. Biology)	Mech. Eng. (incl. Naval Arch. & Textiles)	Electrical Engineering		Civil Engineering	

Ronald Scott, who studied for the degree in the 1940s, said, 'If you're examined by the people who lecture you, I think there's a better chance that the stuff they examine you on will have been well taught by them. The London External wasn't exactly hit-and-miss, but you had to cover a wide range without really knowing what was going to come up in the exams.'

The remote nature of the London External Degree system meant that the only staff members with experience on planning courses were those who had worked with Higher National courses, or who had been involved with courses for professional examinations at degree or honours degree level. What the College needed by the 1960s was degree courses planned and supervised by its own staff. One way of initiating such courses was to seek some form of affiliation with Strathclyde University, but the university itself was lukewarm about the idea, and, again, many Paisley people saw it as another form of submission to a Glasgow institution.

Principal Hugh Henry and the Board of Governors under their Chairman, Robin Elles of J & P. Coats, finally decided, with the SED's encouragement, to seek validation for the College from the newly constituted CNAA (Council for National Academic Awards), which would then empower it to run CNAA degree courses in Engineering and Science.

This presented a new challenge to the staff. Until then, many of them had been accustomed to teaching 'pre-packaged' London University courses – now they were faced with the task of becoming much more involved in planning and supervising courses. Chemistry lecturer Donald Stevenson says that in the 1950s, the College staff had to be flexible – as well as dealing with Chemistry Department students, he himself taught engineering students who required a grasp of chemistry and physics.

'In these days the staff played an enormous part in leading developments within the College. They were dedicated, and they just got on with it, and did what was needed. Professional qualifications were just as important as internal and national qualifications. In the Biology Department, in particular, professional qualifications were considered to be important even before the lecturers were in a position to offer their own biology degree courses.'

As London University had done several decades earlier, the CNAA found staff accommodation, some of the technical facilities and project areas within Paisley College of Technology to be inadequate, and required more space per student in the engineering laboratories. A Planning and Development Committee was set up to consider the College's identity and establish its role in the relationship between academia and industry.

Accommodation was still a major problem; the new extension had been built to specifications drawn up in the 1950s, but since then the College had expanded to five academic departments and was once again in need of more space.

To its credit, the SED quickly responded to the predicament, providing funds for the erection of 12,500 square feet of temporary accommodation, which, with the modification of existing buildings was enough to meet the criteria set by CNAA.

Hugh Henry

After holding the post of Principal for almost 20 years, Hugh Henry retired at the end of the 1965/1966 session.

Hamish MacLachlan, the College's first librarian, remembers him as a 'genial amiable gentleman, very kindly. He always acted on a consensus of staff.' John Paul, a lecturer in Civil Engineering, considered Henry to be, 'A down-to-earth sort of man who knew his staff very well, and knew the name of every cleaner in the place. He didn't interfere – his job was administration, and he got on with it.'

Claud McNeil, who remembers Principal Henry and James Denholm attending auction rooms to buy furniture and equipment for the College during the difficult days before CI status arrived, adds, 'Hugh Henry was a nice bloke in his own way, but it was a shame that Jim Denholm didn't get the Principal's job. He deserved it for services to the College.'

Members of his office staff remember Hugh Henry as a man who retained the 'family feeling', despite the College's growth, and fought for day-release and part-time facilities in order to help those students with the ability to further their education but without privileged circumstances. 'He was very much a driving force where day release was concerned,' says Donald Stevenson. 'He encouraged it a lot, and I think there was also Government encouragement. I believe that the Government departments, such as the SED, had more to do with the changes the College went through than they get credit for.'

Dr Alistair Nicoll of the Department of Chemistry and Chemical Engineering Department came to know Principal Henry as 'a very underestimated man, the man who put Paisley College of Technology on the map. He moved us from being a hole-in-the-wall further education institution to becoming a Central Institution with its own up-to-date laboratories. He was the man who got the money together to build what are now A, B and D Blocks.'

Hugh Henry and Tom Howie in the mid-1950s.

Lecturer Gordon Macaulay thought Principal Henry '. . . superb, but never fully recognised,' while Professor McEwan of the Quality Centre recalls him as 'able and gentlemanly, one of the early energy conservationists. He had the habit of switching off the lights in empty classrooms.' He also remembers Hugh Henry and Miss McNab warning the administrative office staff, 'On no account speak to the students!'

In John Oswald's view, 'Hugh Henry was under-rated as a Principal. He was a blunt man and at times he may have rubbed some people up the wrong way. It was fairly conventional at that time for a retiring Principal to receive an honour of some sort, like an MBE, but Hugh Henry got nothing. In his views on day-release he was ahead of his time . . . after the Second World War, Paisley College of Technology was in the forefront of day-release in Scotland.

'He was very mechanically-minded. He loved working with his hands, and if he wasn't in his office he was usually to be found in the technical workshops, talking to the technicians. I remember once walking round a building-in-progress with him – he loved to talk to the builders about their work.'

Technician Arthur Hughes was impressed by Hugh Henry's administrative ability. 'The College had very little money then, and Principal Henry was very good at making the most of what cash we had. He obtained some donations of equipment through communicating with his students' employers, and every year he encouraged Babcock & Wilcox to send an apprentice to work with the College technicians.' Mr Hughes remembers a Saturday morning class instructed by ICI's chief scientific glass-blower.

George Haig, a former lecturer in the Physics Department, recalls that Principal Henry always invited new staff members to tea in his room. 'You felt like one of the family. In those days we all thought it was a great privilege to be a member of the staff of Paisley College of Technology.'

A distinguished visitor from Malaysia visits the College in the mid 1960s. Left to right; in the foreground, Duncan MacSween, Douglas Armour, Joseph McLean and Principal Henry. Ian Shepherd and Tom Howie can be seen in the background. A considerable number of Malaysian students studied at the College in the early 1960s.

Chapter 6
Principal Edwin Kerr
(1966-1972)

Dr Edwin Kerr, Hugh Henry's successor, was in his fortieth year when he came to Paisley in May 1966. An ambitious and single-minded man, he had been Head of the Mathematics Department at the Royal College of Advanced Technology in Salford, and as a member of the central committee dealing with that College's bid to become the University of Salford, he possessed first-hand experience in the drafting of ordinances and similar constitutional business. He brought with him the firm belief that Paisley College of Technology, too, could eventually aspire to university status.

Principal Kerr

Dr Kerr arrived in Paisley at a time when proposals made to the CNAA for validation of the College's three engineering degrees had been referred back for major revision and re-submission. As has already been pointed out, because the London University degree courses were controlled from outwith the College, general staff experience in the detailed planning of advanced courses was confined to those lecturers who had been involved in the National Certificate Joint Committees. Consultancy work for industry had increased, but at that stage in the life of the College very little research for work for higher degrees was taking place.

CNAA Recognition

Dr Kerr immediately set about guiding the staff and the Board of Governors through the changes necessary for CNAA validation. Appointed a full year before taking up the post, he had spent the time studying his new College and assessing its needs. Not long after arriving in Paisley he presented a strategy paper to the Board of Governors, spelling out the need for commitment to the provision of full-time degree courses; identification of student population targets; provision of accommodation appropriate to a degree-level institution; agreement with the SED on appropriate staffing levels; the need for an Academic Board responsible for academic planning, and expansion of the administrative structure in order to provide the

Robin Elles
Chairman of the
Board of
Governors, 1966-
1974.

necessary support for the College's development.

In 1966, the CNAA approved the College's Honours degrees in Chemistry and Physics and an Ordinary degree in Science. The following year Ordinary and Honours degrees in Civil, Mechanical Engineering and Electrical Engineering and Technology were approved. This constituted a milestone in the College's history, making it one of the first Colleges in the country to offer its own BSc degrees at Ordinary and Honours level.

Dr Kerr's determination to take Paisley College of Technology to the forefront of higher education in Scotland was supported by Robin Elles, who became Chairman of the Board of Governors shortly before Kerr took over as Principal. Elles, a senior manager with J & P Coats, was a Cambridge graduate who had formerly worked in the Sudan and had held high rank in the Sudanese Defence Forces during World War Two. He was competent, confident and capable of taking the lead when necessary – leadership qualities he shared with the new Principal. The two men worked well together, and Elles fully supported the points made in Edwin Kerr's strategy paper.

Administrative Changes

During his final years as Principal, Hugh Henry had established a College Council of Heads of Departments answerable to himself and without any formal relationship with the Board of Governors. Dr Kerr replaced it with an Academic Board consisting of Heads of Departments, Vice-Principal James Denholm and four elected staff members, with the Principal himself as chairman. Because of the growth in the number of departments, they were grouped for consultative purposes into two Schools, one of Engineering, the other of Science.

The Board of Governors' Committees were reorganised as four Standing Committees on Finance, Property, Student Affairs, and Planning and Development, with ad hoc sub-groups as necessary. Each committee had a constitution and regular review, and staff members were co-opted on the joint nomination of the Chairman of the Governors and the Principal.

A further break from local control came in 1967, when the Principals and Chairmen of the Boards of the technological colleges in Paisley, Aberdeen and Dundee constituted themselves as a Standing Committee of the Central Institutions (Technological) with the support of their three Boards of Governors. The committee worked to reach agreement on a common policy on staffing levels, and policy papers on research and library provision (which originated in Paisley College of Technology) were duly produced.

After Hugh Henry's relaxed manner, the new Principal's businesslike way of running College affairs came as a shock to the staff. 'Things changed out of all recognition compared to the mid-fifties,' commented Professor

Kathleen Smith,
Assistant
Secretary Finance,
1968-1989.

Smyth, Head of Biology. 'There were also changes in management style.'

David Duff, for many years a member of the Chemistry Department staff, sums up the new situation. 'The early 1960s was a period of change for the College as well as for higher education in general. October 1963 saw the appearance of the long-awaited Robbins Report on Higher Education, with its implications for Paisley, and this was followed, two days after its publication, by the opening of new College buildings comprising extended accommodation for the Chemistry, Engineering and Physics Departments, as well as a new administrative suite. These were required to cater for the increasing numbers of National Certificate students then attending the College on a day-release basis which, in turn, led to a significant increase in staff appointments. The effects of these developments were to be quite far-reaching in the years following.

'Hitherto, a significant number of the College's staff had come from within, when able students, on completion of (in many cases) external degrees, were offered teaching posts. These were sometimes part-time in the first instance, but subsequently resulted in a transition to full-time appointments. In the early 1960s, however, the additional lectureships created to cope with greater student numbers were filled by increasingly well-qualified persons having no previous connection with the College. They brought with them the experience and knowledge gained either at other academic institutions, or, important for a developing College of Technology, from time spent in industry. A number of these new lecturers possessed higher degrees, and this prompted some existing staff, mainly from the Chemistry Department, to enter part-time study for the PhD degree at the recently created University of Strathclyde. This initiative was encouraged by the Principal and the College authorities, recognising the importance of a highly qualified staff in its future development and expansion.

'As a consequence of these trends, coupled with the creation of new departments and new areas of study such as the Social Sciences, what had up to that time been a compact and close-knit staff with a high level of social intercourse became of necessity more fragmented. Events such as the annual College outing were soon replaced by a number of similar smaller events run by individual departments, and the common staff room by separate departmental meeting-places.'

New Departments

Due to a belief that universities were slow to adapt to the demands of a changing technologically-based society, the Principals of Scotland's Central Institutions felt that there was a case for educating at least some economists, psychologists and sociologists in predominantly technological institutions,

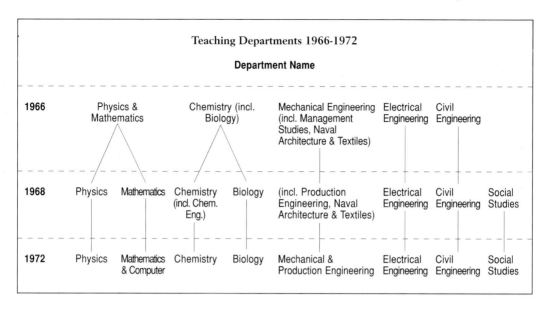

Teaching Departments 1966-1972

Department Name

1966	Physics & Mathematics		Chemistry (incl. Biology)		Mechanical Engineering (incl. Management Studies, Naval Architecture & Textiles)	Electrical Engineering	Civil Engineering	
1968	Physics	Mathematics	Chemistry (incl. Chem. Eng.)	Biology	(incl. Production Engineering, Naval Architecture & Textiles)	Electrical Engineering	Civil Engineering	Social Studies
1972	Physics	Mathematics & Computer	Chemistry	Biology	Mechanical & Production Engineering	Electrical Engineering	Civil Engineering	Social Studies

Harry Sheldon, first Head of Department of Social Studies.

Jim Adams, whose career started in Mechanical Engineering in the 1960s. He retired as Associate Head of Applied Social Studies.

rather than in the Arts faculties of universities. The SED opposed the setting-up of Social Science courses in Paisley, expecting that the increased group of Scottish universities would make ample provision for the subject.

Big Brother Glasgow was still very much in evidence, and opposed to any move on the College's part to take over sub-degree work in commerce and distribution shed by the Scottish College of Commerce.

Conversely, one of CNAA's conditions of approval was that a Department of General Studies should be set up in Paisley, enabling students on science and technology courses to relate their studies to a wider socio-economic context. During the 1966/67 session a Department of General Studies was set up with responsibility for teaching social and economic studies as components of degree, HND and HNC courses. This became the Department of Social Studies.

Lecturers James Adams, Michael Bone and William Elder were transferred to the new department from the Department of Mechanical and Production Engineering, and Harry Sheldon, who had been recruited from Salford by Dr Kerr, took up the post of Head of Social Studies. Other full-time staff members appointed during the first session included David McDowall, author of the thesis on *Technical Education in Paisley 1870-1920* and Chris Madigan. Both men were among

Konrad Hopkins.

Jas Gemmell.

those involved in developing courses in Communication and English studies, mainly for engineering students.

'In general,' David McDowall recalls, 'the engineering staff found it hard to understand why their students should be involved in social studies. They didn't seem to understand that we were providing necessary input to these courses.' Chris Madigan, who came to Paisley from Leeds, agrees. 'Engineers obviously didn't appreciate social sciences . . . the first generation of social scientists were seen as a bit odd!'

Other staff members included Jas Gemmell, Sylvia Clark, (author of *Paisley – a History*, published in 1988) and American Konrad Hopkins, who, on arriving at Dover, informed an immigration officer that he was to teach in Paisley, England. 'No you're not,' came the reply. 'Paisley's in Scotland.'

It was the first of several surprises; having read poems written by Robert Burns in English as part of his English Literature course as an American student, Konrad was under the impression, until he came to Scotland, that Burns was an English poet. He was also surprised by the number of poets Paisley has spawned during its history.

During a varied career, Konrad worked at the Florida State University with a popular young athletics student whose hopes to become a professional footballer were dashed by a serious car crash. When Konrad suggested an acting career instead, as football and acting both require performances before an audience, the student, Burt Reynolds, heeded the advice, and went on to become a well-known film actor.

New Degrees

The CNAA Charter in 1966, which created a new sense of purpose within the College, is described in the booklet *90 Years of Degree Teaching in Chemistry* by Alastair Mitchell as, 'Perhaps the most significant event in the life of the Chemistry and Chemical Engineering Department.' The Charter gave the department, among others, the chance to offer its own BSc degrees, and by 1973, when new chemical engineering laboratories were built, the department had also become the main Scottish centre for teaching and examining the long established Honours level Graduateship examination of the Royal Society of Chemistry.

Other departments benefited from the wind of change, and staff members throughout the College reacted positively to the new challenge. As a result of the Social Work (Scotland) Act of 1968, the College was given permission to plan a social science based degree course in a form that could introduce an eventual professionally recognised option in Social Work.

A degree course in Computing Science, one of the first of its kind in Scotland, commenced during the 1970/1 session, while a School of Social Planning and Management Studies joined the Schools of Engineering and Science.

1972 saw the introduction of the first Ordinary and Honours degrees in Social Studies and an Honours degree in Biology. A professionally-recognised diploma in Land Economics also commenced in 1968, and was upgraded in 1972 to a degree course.

Development of Biology Department

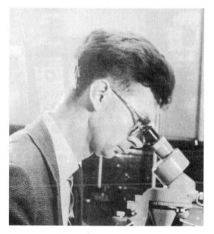

Lecturer J Hamilton at work in the Biology Department c. 1968.

During the early 1960s, Professor Smyth of the Biology Department was involved for a year in a Nuffield Foundation programme to update science in schools, thus acquiring close contacts with secondary education. As a result, the College began developing courses for biology teachers.

The College also played host to the Strathclyde Environmental Education Group (SEEG), working on sample modules for schools. Professor Smyth, who was involved with the study and has since been awarded an Honorary Doctorate by the University for his contribution to environmental education, believes that the College played a considerable and perhaps unrecognised role in the development of environmental education during the 1970s and 1980s. When the Biology Department was first set up in 1955, Professor Smyth was the sole staff member; by the time he retired in 1988 the department had 20 staff members.

The Computers Arrive

Although the Electrical Engineering Department used electronic computers in the 1960s, it was during Principal Kerr's time that the Computer Centre was established, a very significant development considering that there are now many computer labs and several PCs in almost every room in the University.

Alan Wilson, who retired from the Computer Centre in 1996, recalls, 'The first computer was installed in the summer of 1967 in the basement of B Block (C Block, as it was then). A Computer Unit with a staff of two was established, and initially it was an integral part of the Mathematics Department under Tom Gaskell. The hardware configuration consisted of an ICT 1901 processor with 16k memory (ICT became ICL in 1968), a Paper Tape Reader/Punch, and a Paper Tape Punch, at a total cost of £42,550.

'Each job (programme and data) was punched onto 1" wide paper tape using a Teletype 33 machine, which consisted of a keyboard and paper tape reader/punch, and hard copy was printed on a roll of paper.

'As the computer did not include a disk drive, every job processed

Electrical Engineering Lecturer Joe Kinsler with the Solartron HS 7/3 hybrid computer in 'D' Block in the late 1960s.

Computer operator Janis Murray at the ICL Computer in 1973.

involved loading a compiler (on paper tape, of course) followed by tapes containing the programme and data. Even the output was obtained on paper tape, since a printer did not exist. The output tapes obtained by the 1901's paper tape punch were then fed into a Teletype 33 to produce hard-copy printouts. The simplest job took about 20 minutes to process, and programme development was usually a time-consuming and frustrating experience.

'In 1968 a further £30,000 was spent on installing two exchangeable disk units of 4M bytes each, and a line printer. These enhancements significantly reduced the processing time to 2/3 minutes for most jobs.

'By 1969, the staff of the Computer Unit had increased to eight, mainly involved in preparing paper tapes and operating the 1901. The choice of accommodation for the 1901 proved to a be a nightmare on a few occasions. It was sited immediately below a Physics Department laboratory, and on one occasion water leaked into the computer room from equipment left on overnight in the lab above. On the following morning the operators arrived to find themselves ankle-deep in water, and it took several days to dry the 1901 out. After this happened on two further occasions, we installed water detectors and alarms.

'Despite the slow processing times compared to present-day performances, there was plenty of spare capacity during those early years because there were so few computer-users. In an attempt to justify the computer's existence, software was written to process some of the College's commercial work, principally for the payroll, invoicing, and student records systems. They were all written in the Algol programming language, the main computer language used by the staff at that time. A computing service was also provided to most of the secondary schools in the West of Scotland. The schools sent us batches of pupils' programmes by post, written in Algol and usually on scraps of paper, to be punched on paper tape and processed on the 1901. This service to schools lasted until 1973, when Jordanhill College of Education took over the responsibility.

'The teaching of computing in the first few years of the 1901's existence had been confined to very few courses, and involved programming in Algol and the occasional use of some of the applications packages which were bundled in with the hardware. The first students to take the degree in Computing Science (then called BSc in Computing with Operational Research) enrolled in 1970. During the next few years, demand, especially from students on that course, increased considerably; so much so that 2-shift and later 3-shift working by the operations staff became necessary.

'Apart from the 1901's limited capacity, its greatest drawback was that only one programme could be processed at a time. Consequently, we became attracted to the relatively new concept of 'time-sharing', whereby several users could access a computer simultaneously. The 1901 continued to provide a service until 1975, but in the early 1970s we also dabbled with time-sharing systems, namely a PDP-8/E machine and some commercial time-sharing bureaux.'

Paisley Campus –
Green Field or Town Centre?

In 1967, when the College approached the Town Council for planning permission in order to expand, a move to new accommodation on a green belt site at Erskine New Town was suggested as an alternative.

Robin Elles, then Chairman of the Governors, was enthusiastic. It was his view that Paisley Burgh was indifferent towards the College, and he found the idea of a new and spacious campus attractive. He was supported in this by the Convenor of the County Council, Sir James MacFarlane. Stuart Emery, who later became a Governor, feels on looking back that the local authorities of that time were 'perhaps short-sighted in not seeing what the College was doing for Paisley. Local engineering companies were disappearing; and the College was becoming one of the biggest employers in the town.'

The SED showed little interest in the proposal to move to Erskine, but perhaps the Town Council was, after all, aware of the College's growing importance, for it was unhappy about the possibility, and appealed to the Secretary of State who, in 1968, ruled in favour of expansion within Paisley Burgh. If the Scottish Secretary's decision had gone the other way, the College/University might today have boasted a green campus like that of

The views of the President of the SRC on the effect on the College of remaining in Paisley as reported in the *Paisley Daily Express* of November 4th 1970.

PAISLEY DAILY EXPRESS, WEDNESDAY, NOVEMBER 4, 1970.

Development too restricted, says S.R.C. president

COLLEGE IN TOWN COULD NOT GROW TO UNIVERSITY

PAISLEY COLLEGE OF TECHNOLOGY has no prospect of ever gaining university status if it remains in the town, Mr John Hopwood, president of the Students' Representative Council, said yesterday.

Within the town, its expansion will be limited by the amount of land avail-

CHAMPION FOR

'High Church Halls' were known to generations of Paisley students. Now part of Oakshaw Trinity Church, the expansion of the 1990s has meant that they are still in use as lecture halls.

The former Paisley Cattle Market in Storie Street. The Mary Brough Hall used for lectures is now demolished. It was situated on the same side of the street.

the University of Stirling – but the town of its birth would have been the poorer for its loss.

As a result of this ruling, an area of 11.5 acres bounded by George Street, Lady Lane, High Street and Weighhouse Close was re-zoned for educational use. Renfrew County Council objected, and plans were laid for a public enquiry. A date was fixed, but the principal objectors withdrew at the eleventh hour. Once the matter was decided, the College, which had agreed with the Town Council to avoid compulsory purchase orders, began to negotiate the purchase of land from Priorscroft Bowling Club, Paisley Co-operative Manufacturing Society, the owners of the Cattle Market, and other properties within the designated area.

A multi-phased development was planned, the first three phases to comprise of accommodation for; 1) Civil and Mechanical Engineering; 2) the Library, Social Studies, Mathematics and Electrical Engineering; and 3) Biology and Physics. Phase 4 was intended as accommodation for social and communal activities, including a much-needed Students' Union.

Former University Librarian Hamish Maclachlan affirms that Edwin Kerr, eager to expand College premises, had considered various options, one of them involving the acquisition of land on the opposite side of High Street, and building the proposed new library on the site of John Neilson School, with residences for the Librarian and Heads of Departments on the top floor. 'Fortunately,' says Mr Maclachlan, 'this proposal came to naught.' The library, which opened in 1976, was eventually sited in the Elles Building.

During construction of the new buildings, class accommodation had to be leased where available. Chris Madigan, who joined the staff of Applied Social Studies in 1969, recalls that his department was 'dotted around' in the 1960s and early 1970s. 'Initially we were in G Block, then at Westerfield (the Victorian house bought as a stop-gap in 1955). Then we moved to the Co-op Funeral Hall. The filing cabinets were kept in the mortuary area.' It is perhaps appropriate that Social Studies Lecturer, the Rev Jack Dale, was located in the area of the hall that had formerly been a chapel.'

Chris Madigan.

Joseph Kinsler, who began lecturing in the Electrical and Electronic Engineering Department in 1965, also remembers taking classes in the funeral hall, and, at one time, in an old church hall adjoining the Cattle Market. 'I had to lecture to the sound of mooing cattle; they were pretty loud, and not very selective in their timing.'

One of the standard jokes among students in those days was that they had to check to see which denominations were on their timetables, and John Oswald, when College Secretary, recalls being told by Bill Lawson, a senior lecturer in Land Economics, 'If you can get me a class in an RC church, I'll have an ecumenical set.'

Relations with Industry

Like his predecessor, Dr Kerr recognised the benefits of the Industrial Liaison Centre from the first, and continued to support it. When he became a lecturer in the Civil Engineering Department in 1963, John Paul was 'amazed' at the number of contacts between the College and industry. 'Industrialists weren't averse to phoning and saying, "We have a wee problem. Can we come in and discuss it with you?"'

By 1967, the Industrial Liaison workload had become so heavy that John Wylie, an organic chemist who had earlier studied for his HNC at Paisley Technical College, was appointed as second Industrial Liaison Officer, working with John Oswald, who at that time was still the Senior Industrial Liaison Officer.

He saw his remit as providing help to companies, using the best possible sources. 'That could be, for instance, NEL, the Rubber and Plastics Association in England, or one of the universities – there was a network. But in practice, John Oswald and I found that in about 80-90% of the enquiries, the help could be provided by Paisley College of Technology.'

In 1967, the relative success of the Industrial Liaison Centres within Scotland's five Central Institutions led to the setting-up of similar centres in England and Wales. The Ministry of Technology then took on the funding of CI centres from the SED, later handing the task over to the Department of Trade and Industry. Also by 1967 a Technical Intelligence Service had evolved as part of the Industrial Liaison scheme, whereby the College's staff, where possible, provided no-cost or low-cost solutions to technical problems experienced by small businesses. The benefits of this for the academic staff lay in the opportunity to solve 'live' problems, as well as some trade-offs in information regarding the location and availability of materials and equipment for College use. Thus, as Dr Graham points out in his thesis, the College cultivated a 'can do' approach to requests for help.

Low Cost Automation Centre

Visiting an automation laboratory in Delft during a delegation tour of Holland in 1966, ILO John Oswald came across a Low Cost Simulator – a hydraulic/pneumatic rig that demonstrated ways in which simple low cost devices could speed up production systems. Shortly after his return to Scotland, the Ministry of Technology offered to finance training in Low Cost Automation techniques. The College then persuaded the Ministry of Technology to purchase the simulator, and bring it to Paisley to help create a Low Cost Automation Centre. Sam Monaghan (Mechanical Engineering) and Archie McKenzie (Electrical Engineering) devoted a great deal of time and energy to establishing the LCAC, which enabled the College to study the way in which various firms operated, provide consultancy and advice on low cost automation and training (including a library of trade literature) and, eventually, to build prototypes for customers. A similar centre was set up at the Heriot-Watt University in Edinburgh to serve the east of Scotland. Sam Monaghan, says John Wylie, 'was one of the Centre's major technical experts, and did a lot of work out among industrial companies.'

Sam Monaghan lectures in the Low Cost Automation Centre in the late 1960s. A former Paisley student and external London University graduate, Mr Monaghan is now Associate Head of the Department of Mechanical and Manufacturing Engineering.

The Low Cost Automation Rig.

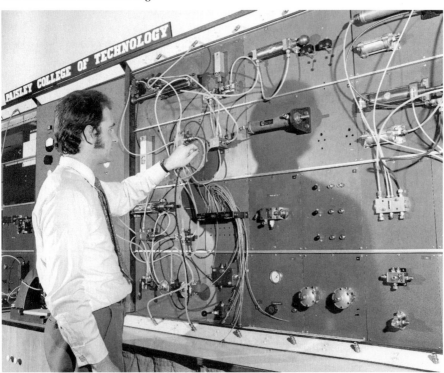

Industrial Units

By 1968, thanks to the LCAC, the College's role in industrial liaison had moved far beyond the original conception of 1963. During the 1960s, for instance, the Department of Mechanical and Production Engineering's special expertise in welding technology and non-destructive testing of welds had been directed into a series of short courses for industry. This was to lead to the setting up in 1974 of the Scottish School of Non-Destructive Testing and ultimately the Quality Centre.

Demands from the construction industry for the College's testing services, started in the Civil Engineering Department on a fee-earning basis in the late 1950s, grew to such an extent over the next decade that in 1970

Mr Eric Downey, for many years Director of MACDATA.

the Materials and Components Development and Testing Association (MACDATA) began to function as a self-financing unit. Director Bob Hardy supervised the managerial and technical staff and by the end of the 1970s the unit was handling more than 600 contracts per annum with a fee income turnover of £102,000.

One of MACDATA's main lines has always been window-testing, a big growth area in the 1970s. 'We are still the only place in Scotland to do commercial window-testing,' says M. Arthur, the current Director. 'Two test rigs built here were used to develop the method which eventually became a national testing standard, formulated in conjunction with BSI

Window testing at MACDATA.

(the British Standards Institute) in the late 1960s and early 1970s. The principal test then, as today, was for weather-tightness.'

In general, tests carried out in the MACDATA laboratories fall into three categories – Structural Testing carried out on beams, concrete, steel or timber units to check load-bearing properties, Material Testing, and testing fluid groups. Most of the tests are carried out in the on-campus laboratories, but some are dealt with on-site.

The valuable experience gained by the lecturers from the consultancy/testing work is used in 'feedback' for the benefit of students. 'MACDATA is an important element in the relationship between the Civil Engineering Department and industry,' says lecturer John Paul. 'Occasionally classes are brought in as observers, thus combining academic teaching with industrial projects.'

Social Studies Units

In 1971 a Local Government Research Unit (LGRU) was set up, with assistance from the College and a project-related grant from the Rowntree Trust, as an extension of the Department of Social Studies.

Throughout the 1970s, LGRU, which aspired to develop as a national centre for Scotland (conducting research into local government processes

Specialist units in 1985. Related Departments highlighted. (Based on a report on industrial liaison prepared by J. Wylie c. 1983).

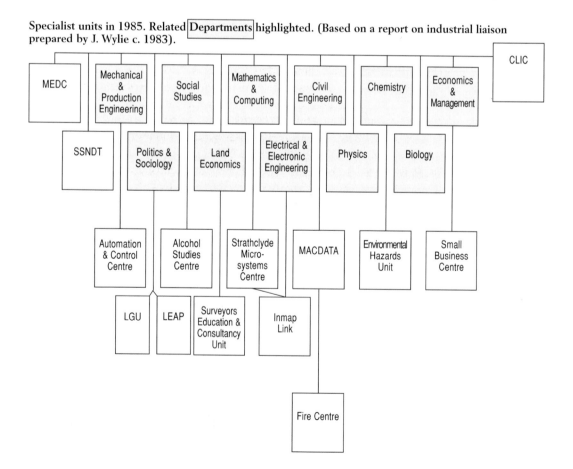

and issues, promoting new ideas and providing a resource facility for local government organisations) attracted grant aid from the Scottish Home and Health Department. It undertook a number of research studies, issued a series of research and working papers, and promoted conferences and seminars, but low funding held it back, and by 1980 it faced an uncertain future.

In the early 1970s, staff in Social Studies also created a special unit known as Management and Planning Services (MAPS) to provide consultancy services based on management skills and applied economics. MAPS survived for only a few years, providing consultancy mainly in work study.

In general, throughout the 1960s, 70s and 80s, as the diagram opposite shows, there was a considerable growth in the number of centres and units attached to College departments. These provided practical links with industry and outside bodies which enhanced the College's reputation and benefited staff and students alike.

Student Life

By 1969, the full-time student population had reached 700, and it had been agreed with the SED that in another 10 years' time, that figure would reach 2,000, although Dr Kerr himself thought that by then, the figure would be nearer 3,000.

The SED had agreed to allocate funds for refurbishment of a Students' Union if suitable accommodation could be found, but the hunt was still on for a venue. In the meantime, the students were coping as best they could with limited facilities, and still – as their President pointed out in *Impact*, published by the SRC – had to rely on the generosity of the Governors for funds, because their own constitution had no legal standing.

Late in 1969, the SED approved the conversion of property in Weighhouse Close into a Students' Union, but, disappointingly, the building was then found to be structurally unsound. When the Governors then suggested that Union premises could be sited on top of an existing College building, the students, who contemptuously called the suggestion a 'pigeon-loft project', staged a sit-in in the refectory, depriving the staff of their lunch.

Not long afterwards, a new Union site was found in the former Department of Employment buildings in Hunter Street. They were already too small to hold the growing number of students, but were considered to be better than nothing. In view of its former use, the students dubbed their new Union 'The B'roo', a local interpretation of 'Bureau'. In the following year the College bought the former Peter Brough Home for Nurses at Oakshaw for use as a students' residence, naming it the Brough Residence.

There was also a grievance over the lack of representation for students on the Academic Board and the Board of Governors. Feelings ran so high that in February 1969 a call for militant student action on the matter was

Left: Miss Maureen H. Gray, Mr. Raj Desai, Veena Patel, Mr. Nitin Doshi and Mr. Bill Tennant.

TECHNICAL COLLEGE STUDENTS' CABARET

The Paisley Technical College held a Students' Cabaret recently in Paisley.

Photographs by Stephens Orr

Right: Tap dancers Helen and Janet.

The Country Girls, Miss Maureen Moreland, Miss Angela Hodd, Miss Lindsay Kelly and Miss Mandy Anderson.

Miss Effie Drummond.

Right: A touch of make-up from Miss Sheila Guthrie.

Left: The Folk Element.

Three Scottish Country Dance Girls, Bonny, Christine and Jean, with the Piper, Mr. Brennan.

A student social event recorded in 1968 in the pages of the *Glasgow Illustrated.*

The B'roo. The Students'
Union in Hunter Street.

The Brough Residence. The home for nurses opened
by Princess Louise on the same day that she laid the
foundation stone of the Technical School became a
College Residence in 1971.

The interior of the B'roo in the 1970s.

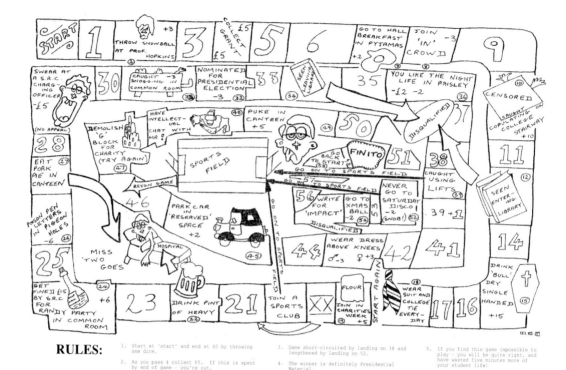

RULES:

1. Start at 'start' and end at 60 by throwing one dice.

2. As you pass 4 collect £5. If this is spent by end of game - you're out.

3. Game short-circuited by landing on 38 and lengthened by landing on 52.

4. The winner is definitely Presidential Material.

5. If you find this game impossible to play - you will be quite right, and have wasted five minutes more of your student life!

'The PCT Association Game' from a students' magazine printed in 1970.

narrowly defeated. Dr Kerr, who attended the meeting, gave his support to the request for a Students' Union and agreed that the SRC President be allowed to attend the Board of Governors' next meeting as an observer. The Board then agreed that suitable premises for social and indoor recreational student use should be given top priority in the College's development plan.

In the following month, after a meeting between students' representatives and Principals of Scotland's Colleges of Technology, *Impact* (the name came from 'I'M PAisley College of Technology') reported that Paisley had 'by far the greatest degree of student representation in College government.'

Although full-time students now predominated, the College's history had mainly involved part-time students. Because of this, and because many later students came from homes with little or no previous experience of higher education, the institution had, over the years, developed a tradition of strong student support through effective teaching. A tutorial system was built into all courses at a time when this was a relative rarity on science and technological courses.

The general changes in administration during the 1960s saw a full-time Appointments Officer replacing the former part-time service, a move which resulted, in 1979, in a comprehensive Students' Advisory Service. J Horrocks, a former textiles lecturer was the first Director. In 1967 a Graduates and Former Students' Association was formed, but this never achieved the success which today's Alumni Association enjoys.

Changes and Expansion

In 1969/70, Paisley's new Municipal Buildings were opened, a central shopping piazza was built over a section of the River Cart, and the old County Square buildings in Gilmour Street were demolished.

Developments were also afoot in the College. During the 1970/1 session, the students gained two 'firsts' – their Union building, and a sabbatical President – a full-time official enabled, with financial support, to take a year off the study programme to concentrate on attending to student needs. However, there were still no facilities for physical recreation. Sports fields had been leased from J & P Coats at Millarston, but when the lease ended in 1970 it was not renewed. Until 1980, the students had to use public sports fields.

Ceremonials

At the College's first graduation ceremony in July 1969, Dr Kerr 'capped' 33 BSc students and awarded 33 diplomas to engineering students. 'In the past,' he said during the ceremony, 'the many graduates from the College were the result of successes in the London University external examinations, and as such were graduates of London University rather than the College. This situation is now remedied .'

Graduation ceremonies had been held in the Brough Hall but, as the numbers of graduates increased, the Hall became too small and the ceremony was moved to Paisley Town Hall, with the fifth graduation being held there in 1973. The Duke of Edinburgh, then President of CNAA, conferred the awards. Principal Kerr attended in his new role as Chief Executive of the CNAA.

Sohan S Bhopal of the School of Engineering is presented with the Watt Medal by Mrs Watson in a Brough Hall graduation.

The presentation of
ceremonial robes in memory
of Dr Watt. Left to right:
Mrs Watson (Dr Watt's
niece), Principal Kerr,
Robin Elles, Miss Watt (Dr
Watt's sister).

Edwin Kerr, who was by this time
Chief Officer of the CNAA, with
H.R.H. the Duke of Edinburgh at
the Town Hall graduation 1973.

College graduation in Paisley Town Hall in the presence of H.R.H. The Duke of Edinburgh.

John Witherspoon Bicentenary

Another ceremonial event held in October 1968 involved a link with America's Princeton University, when a number of functions were held in Paisley to honour John Witherspoon DD, who had ministered at the town's Laigh Kirk in the eighteenth century.

The Rev. J. Witherspoon

In 1768, Witherspoon, who held Doctorates in Philosophy from both Edinburgh and St Andrews Universities, was invited to become President of the then-struggling New Jersey College in America, now Princeton University. Over the years he developed the College, and made his name known throughout America. He became the first Moderator of the American General Assembly, and was influential in drawing up its Confession of Faith and Order of Service. He was the only educationalist and clergyman to sign the American Declaration of Independence on July 4th, 1776.

Paisley College of Technology identifies strongly with the sturdy Scottish teaching ethics which Witherspoon introduced into what was then known as the New World. The 200th anniversary of his arrival in America was celebrated by a joint commemorative service in St George's Church (the former Laigh Kirk) with a live transatlantic link-up between the church and Princeton University's College Chapel. The Provost, Magistrates and Councillors of Paisley Burgh then presided over a buffet tea in the College's Brough Hall. On the following day, there was a memorial lecture in the College on Witherspoon's life and work, followed by a dinner.

In a talk given during the celebrations, Henry Patterson, Mayor of Princeton, said that John Witherspoon had formed America's first debating society, where two of his favourite subjects – freedom and independence – were often discussed.

Farewells

Several associations, both industrial and personal, ended during Dr Kerr's time as Principal.

End of the Textile Courses

In 1971, a general decline in the number of students taking textile subjects in Scottish Colleges caused the SED to decide that all textile education should henceforth be based at the Scottish College of Textiles (SCOT) in Galashiels.

Since the textile industry had played a major part in Paisley's history and the subject had been taught from the College's earliest days (and was still taught to employees of 18 local textile firms) both the Town Council and the College Governors appealed against the decision to the Secretary of State for Scotland and to Paisley MP John Robertson.

The appeals, however, were unsuccessful, and the College's final textile class was held in May 1972. The fate of the textile equipment is not clear; Dr F. Kidd, formerly of SCOT, recalls that the only Paisley machinery of interest to Galashiels was a cotton carding machine used for J & P Coats' trainees, while Mr G. Miller, a former lecturer at the Galashiels College, says that due to lack of time and resources Galashiels could not continue to provide Coats with the service they had received from Paisley. 'It appeared to me that Paisley's Textile Department was operating almost as an adjunct to Coats' Personnel and Training Department,' he said recently.

Dr Alistair Nicoll of the Chemical Engineering Department recalls the days when the present Chemical Engineering Labs, once the Textile Department, 'were full of looms and beaming machines.'

Kenneth Caldwell

The increased overall pressure brought to bear on the administration staff under Dr Kerr's regime had caused problems for Secretary Kenneth Caldwell, who suffered from poor health. When, in 1969, it was decided that someone else should be appointed to take over some of Mr Caldwell's duties, Industrial Liaison Officer John Oswald applied for the post, and became College Secretary. John Wylie, who had joined John Oswald in the

Industrial Liaison Service in 1968, became Senior Industrial Liaison Officer, and Kenneth Caldwell took over the post of Assistant Secretary, dealing with the personnel side of the job.

Kenneth Caldwell was the College's first full-time Senior Administrator, a post which he filled admirably. He was an able and intelligent man, who brought a thoroughly professional attitude to the post of College Secretary, and competently laid the groundwork for those following him to build on.

Hamish Maclachlan, College Librarian at the time, describes Kenneth Caldwell as a 'very helpful man with a convincing, authoritarian manner – so much so that once when he drove me the wrong way up a one-way street, I was in such awe of him as to assume that he had been given special permission from the police to do so.'

James Denholm

In 1969, Vice-Principal James Denholm retired. Like his father, he had devoted most of his life to the College, and many colleagues and students praise his courtesy, kindness and ability.

Lecturer Ronald Scott says, 'He was a very good lecturer, and he did everything without notes, which was quite remarkable. I believe he taught the whole course, up to final year physics from matriculation. Everybody did everything, then.'

'When you got to know him, you appreciated the worth of the man,' says Gordon Macaulay, adding that Jim Denholm was also noted for his absent-mindedness. 'His wife used to check that his socks were at least the same colour before he left in the morning.'

John Oswald remembers an occasion when James Denholm, giving a Saturday morning lecture, was told that someone was waiting for an interview. 'Jim asked for the man to be shown to his office, then finished the lecture and went home, completely forgetting about the interview. At about three o'clock that afternoon the police arrived at his house to say that someone had been spotted at a College window, trying to get out.'

As has been seen already, James Denholm played an important part in gaining Central Institution status for Paisley, and he was foremost among those instrumental in persuading former students to return as staff members. Asked about his future plans during an interview given to *Impact*, the student magazine, a year before retiring, he said, 'Many have said that retirement offered them an opportunity to do the things they wanted to. I have always done this.'

James Denholm died in 1989.

Dr Edwin Kerr.

In 1972, Principal Edwin Kerr resigned his post in order to take up an appointment as the chief executive of CNAA.

A man of great ability, he had, during his six years as Principal, supervised one of the major milestones in the College's history – CNAA recognition. This led to the introduction of new courses and new departments, in particular Social Studies. He streamlined College administration, and prepared the ground for the day when it would aspire to university status. As well as steering the institution through the student boom and the aftermath of the Robbins Report, he had overseen the continuation of the new building programme commenced in his predecessor's time.

Like Hugh Henry, Dr Kerr had recognised the benefits of close collaboration between the College, industry and commerce, and encouraged its development at a time of industrial change in the Paisley and West of Scotland. This resulted in the expansion of some courses and the creation of units such as the Low Cost Automation Centre. He had instigated the College's Disciplinary Procedure, and had given the students a Disciplinary Code which enabled them, in general, to take on responsibility for disciplining themselves.

Tom Gaskell
Head of the
Department of
Mathematics and
Computing and
for some time
Vice-Principal.

He also encouraged his staff to undertake formal research for higher degrees and to acquire membership of appropriate professional institutions. And he had introduced new blood into the College by inviting several former colleagues from the new University of Salford to join him in Paisley, among them Harry Sheldon of Social Studies and Tom Gaskell of Mathematics. This group of able lecturers came to be known collectively (and affectionately) within the College as the 'Salford Mafia.'

Gordon Macaulay remembers Dr Kerr as 'a hard task-master who drove himself as hard as he drove his staff. Few got to know him well, as he was slightly aloof, socially.' He appeared ill at ease when attending staff social functions.

In the view of Professor Smyth of the Biology Department, 'Edwin Kerr had a very powerful effect on the College. He was a turning point, and had the capacity to defuse situations. He was a past-master at taking the heat out of arguments and superb at getting progress out of an impasse.'

'He was one of the best-organised men I knew,' says John Oswald, the former ILO who became College Secretary while Dr Kerr was Principal. 'He was very disciplined, with a first-class brain – the right man in the right place. 1969 and 1970 in particular were exciting years for the College. The development plans were coming along and we had to fight for every single building we got. I learned a lot from Dr Kerr while he was Principal.'

He recalls a train journey that he made to Aberdeen during his time as College Secretary, in the company of Dr Kerr and Robin Elles, who was '. . . a very gentlemanly man. Dr Kerr worked throughout the journey to Aberdeen, and on the way back he went up the platform ahead of us, looking for an empty compartment where he could continue working on the way home. As we followed, Robin Elles asked, "Do you take a dram, John?" and when I admitted that I had been known to, he said, "Thank God for that," and steered me towards the refreshment coach. We finally caught up with Dr Kerr round about Arbroath.'

Former Librarian Hamish Maclachlan remembers Dr Kerr's request to the Board of Governors for a suitable car be put at his disposal. They offered him a Rover 3000, which he refused on the grounds that the College Librarian drove one, and therefore nothing less than a Jaguar would do for the Principal.

'That was one occasion,' Mr Maclachlan comments, 'when I accidentally won Dr Kerr's goodwill.'

Three Principals. Left to right: Principals Kerr, Howie and Henry.

Chapter 7
Principal Tom Howie
(1972-1986)

Edwin Kerr was succeeded as Principal of Paisley College of Technology by the Vice-Principal and Head of Civil Engineering, Tom Howie. Born in Renfrew, he was educated at Renfrew High School and Camphill School in Paisley before taking his London External degree at the College. He then worked for the Clyde Trust Authority before returning to the College as a lecturer, at the request of James Denholm.

Principal Howie.

Following in his predecessor's footsteps, Tom Howie encouraged active participation among his staff within their professional institutions. He himself held high office in the Institution of Civil Engineers, and for a number of years, as Chairman of the Committee of Principals and Directors of Central Institutions, he was involved with developments affecting the higher education system as a whole. He also served for a time on the Council of the CNAA.

New Departments and Courses

Tom Howie also inspired, encouraged and presided over the development of courses and departments within the College.

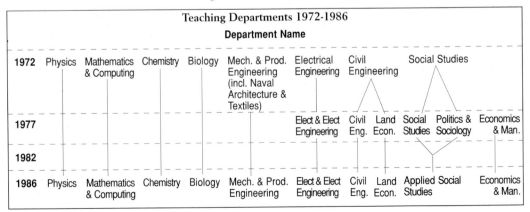

Teaching Departments 1972-1986										
Department Name										
1972	Physics	Mathematics & Computing	Chemistry	Biology	Mech. & Prod. Engineering (incl. Naval Architecture & Textiles)	Electrical Engineering	Civil Engineering		Social Studies	
1977						Elect & Elect Engineering	Civil Eng.	Land Econ.	Social Studies	Politics & Sociology	Economics & Man.
1982										
1986	Physics	Mathematics & Computing	Chemistry	Biology	Mech. & Prod. Engineering	Elect & Elect Engineering	Civil Eng.	Land Econ.	Applied Social Studies	Economics & Man.

Lecturer David Martin with Land Economics students.

1970s Civil Engineering students stream gauging on a field trip to Wiston Lodge near Biggar.

Diversification

During the 1970s, existing courses leading to professional qualifications for the institutes of Biology, Chemistry and Physics were upgraded and expanded at post-qualification level, and postgraduate study for PhD by research was introduced. The College achieved one of its primary aims – diversification beyond its original science and technology base, mainly through growth in Social Sciences.

The SED's policy was that all degree courses should be validated by the CNAA or by an appropriate university, or lead to qualification by a recognised professional body. In Paisley's case, the CNAA validation was granted to all new degree courses and recognition for the professional courses was obtained from the appropriate institutions.

Land Economics

Land Economics originated as a section within the Civil Engineering Department, during Tom Howie's time as Head of Department. Led by Bill Lawson, a surveyor and lawyer, the section was mainly staffed by men who had gained extensive experience in the world of commerce before moving into higher education. In 1966 the College had gained approval from the SED to run a part-time course preparing students for the examinations of the Royal Institution of Chartered Surveyors (RICS) general practice division. In the 1969/70 session, a full-time diploma in Land Economics started, with successful students from the course meriting full exemption from the RICS exams. In 1972, CNAA approved a BSc degree course in Land Economics (a four-year 'thin sandwich' course, converted in 1974 into a 'thick sandwich' course). Not long after 1972, Land Economics became a separate department, with Professor Sandy McIndoe as part-time Head of Department. When he retired in 1978, Professor McIndoe was replaced by Professor Alan Millington. Will Fraser, who had left Paisley in 1983 to lecture at the City University in London, returned to take up the post of Head of the Department in 1986, when Alan Millington moved to Australia.

Law teaching, started by Bill Lawson in the early 1970s, has been expanded. Now, as well as teaching law within the Department, a staff of five lawyers also provide teaching for a range of courses throughout the University, principally in business-related subjects, construction and social studies.

Social Studies

In his 1974/75 report, Principal Howie named Social Studies as the largest department in the College. In addition to offering the BA course in Social Studies, it contributed substantially to BSc courses in Engineering with Marketing and in Land Economics, as well as providing service teaching in all other degree courses offered by the College.

In 1975 a Certificate of Health Visiting and a Diploma for Careers Advisors were introduced, and teaching, training and, ultimately, research into alcohol-related problems resulted in 1978 in the formation of the Alcohol Studies Centre, with a post-qualification diploma validated by CNAA and recognised as an approved course of post-professional training.

Politics and Sociology

In 1982 the establishment of the Department of Politics and Sociology made Paisley College of Technology the only CI in the West of Scotland offering courses in politics, sociology and social studies.

Professor John Foster of the Department of Applied Social Studies who joined the College in 1981.

Given the success of these courses, it came as a severe shock to staff and students when Alex Fletcher, then the Conservative Government's Scottish Education Minister, called for the phasing out of the College's Politics and Sociology Department, and its Social Studies Department, over a four-year period. Although the College authorities had hoped to increase the student intake in these departments, the Government wanted an immediate 50% reduction.

The reaction was swift. Paisley students picketed the Scottish Office in Edinburgh and formed a human chain around the College buildings, while David Steel, then leader of the Liberal Party, tabled a written question in the House of Commons calling for a change of policy.

Eventually a compromise over the threatened departments was reached with the SED, whereby the Department of Politics and Sociology and the Department of Social Studies were combined to become the Department of Applied Social Studies.

Economics and Management

In view of Social Studies' multi-disciplinary nature and increasing size, Principal Howie announced that an additional Department of Economics and Management was to be created from it. Professor Alistair Young, Head of Economics and Management, takes up the story.

Professor Alistair Young of the Department of Economics and Management.

'I came to Paisley in January 1974, joining the Department of Social Studies under Harry Sheldon. This department had a group of people teaching business subjects, under the supervision of the then Associate Head of Department, Michael Crew. He left just a few months later, and is now a distinguished academic in America. When he left, an important decision was taken to split the Department of Social Studies by forming a new department – the Department of Economics and Management.

'They were heavily involved in the early 1970s in the Engineering with Marketing degree then run by the Department of Social Studies; and were also involved in the endeavour to launch the BA Marketing degree. The latter, however, ran into difficulties, mainly because the CNAA considered it to be "too narrowly vocational," and pressed for a slightly broader "Business Economics with Marketing" degree.

'The first Professor of Economics and Management was Peter Sloan, who joined the department around October 1975. About this time, the staff consisted of Peter Sloan, Head of Department, one senior lecturer, Neil Hood, and ten or so lecturers drawn from the mainly business-orientated people of the original Department of Social Studies.

'The Engineering with Marketing degree, originally inherited from Social Studies, eventually fizzled out through lack of student enrolments. It was popular with employers, but students felt that the engineering component was not large enough for them to achieve chartered status. However, by September 1976, the Department of Economics and Management had been given the "green light" by the CNAA to launch the Business Economics with Marketing degree. This new CNAA degree created the opportunity for a certain level of flexibility; i.e., Business Economics could be packaged with options other than Marketing, such as Manpower Studies/Finance/European Economy with Languages, and Management Science.

'The European Economy with Languages option, which proved very popular with the students, was a very easy way for the Department to grow.'

The first graduates from the Department of Economics and Management were in 1980, these students having entered Paisley in about 1975/76. Professor Young recollects that seventeen of these students had taken the Marketing option, and sixteen the Manpower option.

Contribution of the Teaching Staff

The developments described above were achieved with the active participation of the teaching staff . According to Professor Young, 'Paisley has succeeded because of the fairly liberal system of governance practised by successive senior managers. This focuses on the department as a major decision-making centre when it comes to such things as, for example, course development. In other institutions there has been either a rigid system of rules to work by, or, perhaps because the institutions have been larger, or owe more to local authority control – a more hierarchical system with a less flat structure than Paisley.

'Paisley's structure consists of Principal, Head of Department, and members of staff, at least as far as the academic side is concerned. While that has its disadvantages – especially for Heads of Department with staffs of about 70 – the direct contact, both between Head of Departments and staff and Principal and Head of Department, has been much to Paisley's benefit, and certainly has made it in many ways a very pleasant place to work.' This was helped by alterations made in 1973 to the College's constitution which brought academics and student representatives on to the Board of Governors. They were also involved in the Academic Board and its Committees.

Many staff members became active in their professional institutions. Other staff served on CNAA committees and boards, while a number of senior staff became external examiners within higher education throughout the UK. Paisley was well represented on the joint course co-ordinating committee formed by the SED in 1972 and Ken Donaldson and Douglas

Armour in particular, played a significant role for many years on the Central Institutions' staff negotiation body, being commended for their submissions to the Robbins Committee in 1962/63 and the Houghton Commission in 1973/74.

When the title of Professor was introduced in 1974, the Board of Governors, after taking advice, felt that it should be bestowed selectively. The Heads of Departments, however, did not agree; their argument, supported by Principal Howie, was that the title should be given to them all. The Board conceded the point, thus averting ill-feeling and resentment among the staff.

When the Houghton Report on salaries for non-University teachers came out, the Heads of Departments again united to claim that all should be placed on a common salary point regardless of departmental size. Again, they won their case, making Paisley College of Technology unique among the CIs.

Development of the Research Programme

A good example of the active involvement of all levels of staff in the progress of the College was the development of research activities.

The Rochester Report of 1973 had stressed the need for CNAA courses in Colleges to be supported by appropriate levels of research, thus leading to recognition by Research Councils of CNAA degrees. While concurring with the report, the SED required such research on the part of its CIs to be applied, and directly supportive of the work of the undergraduate courses.

Professor T. George Truscott

Professor George Truscott.

Research work in the Department of Chemistry was strongly encouraged by Professor T. George Truscott when he became Head of the Department in 1974. Under his direction, the Department became internationally recognised as a major contributor in the field of Photobiological Chemistry with special emphasis on drugs used in cancer phototherapy.

In 1990, Professor Truscott moved from Paisley to Keele University, where he eventually became Head of the School of Science and Engineering. In a letter written in 1996 he said, 'I spent 16 happy years at Paisley, and much of my current research work was initiated there in collaboration with Professors Sinclair and Roach, Drs Keir, MacLennan, and Forbes, Mrs Ross and Mr Stirling. A wide range of "in bred" students passed through my group, and without these I would have achieved little.'

The Development of Vanish

Vanish, a cleansing preparation to be found in most kitchens, was another example of College-based research.

In the early 1980s the managing director of a Skelmorlie company

Dr Alastair Nicoll.

contacted Paisley College of Technology's Industrial Liaison Centre. He had been impressed by an Australian patent stain-remover called Magic Soap, and wanted to know if a similar stain-remover could be manufactured in the UK. The Chemistry Department took up the challenge, and after identifying the Magic Soap ingredients, staff member Stuart Harvey managed to alter one, thus avoiding any breach of patent.

Because of previous patent problems, the work was carried out on a private consultancy basis under an agreement that included payment to the College. Mixing vessels from the Skelmorlie premises were installed in the flame-proofed area of the Chemical Engineering laboratory, and after the first large-scale batch of Vanish additive was produced, a soap manufacturer made it into soap. Seven months from the day the College had first been approached, Vanish was on the supermarket shelves, and destined to become a staple item in every kitchen.

'The timing was reckoned to be miraculous,' says Dr Alastair Nicoll, now a Senior Lecturer in the Department. 'It was a fascinating experience. Basically we have divided the world into two – in South-east Asia and Australia there is Magic Soap, and in Europe there is Vanish.'

Vanish was later bought over by an American company then sold again, to a large German concern.

George Haig, the Planetarium, and the "Haig Mount"

Although the Physics Department had developed an astronomy-astrophysics course as part of a CNAA degree, the first College planetarium was built by lecturer George Haig, out of paper and ribbed cardboard, for summer in-service teacher-training courses. A second model was made of plywood, and, finally, a more ambitious model was built by George Haig and Ron Williamson, chief technician, for Coats Observatory. Due to a shortage of funds, the Observatory could not at first house the planetarium, and by the time it was installed, George Haig had retired.

'In the early 1960s,' he recalls, 'the College was given the opportunity to buy Coats Observatory, as Paisley Town Council were worried about the cost of financing it. Several College staff members, including Jim Denholm and myself, went to see it, and were highly impressed. Sadly, at that time the College did not have the available funding to buy the Observatory, and no astronomy course to justify the purchase. When we later developed our astronomy course,' George recalls with regret, 'we thought of how close the College had come to owning the Observatory.'

There was a small fibreglass observatory on the roof of C Building for some time, but not much use was made of it because of pressures of time, and the uncertainty of the Scottish weather. It was eventually damaged in a storm.

In the early 1970s, George, a Fellow of the Royal Astronomical Society, designed an instrument known as the Hinge Mount, sometimes called the

George Haig of the Department of Physics with students and planetarium.

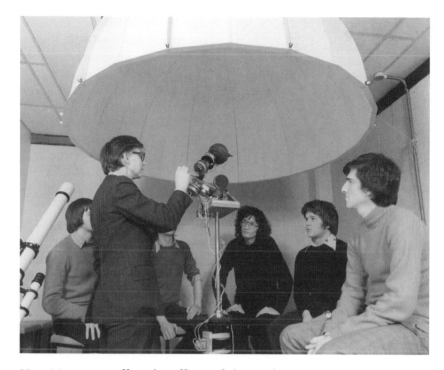

Haig Mount, to offset the effects of the earth's rotation in astronomical photography. The Mount, featured in Patrick Moore's highly successful television series on astronomy, is still in use. In conjunction with Principal Tom Howie, George also patented a machine to demonstrate wave motion. Chief technician Ron Williamson was involved in that project, and the machine was made by disabled ex-servicemen at Erskine Hospital, mainly for export.

As a result of these and other projects, the 1976 CNAA review had special praise for Paisley College of Technology's success in research and related activities. By then, it was receiving £150,000 in financial support from research councils, Government agencies and industrial sponsors, outwith its consultancy earnings.

Relations with Industry
CLIC

In 1971, the Bolton Committee had recommended that Government funding for the Industrial Liaison Service should be replaced by a national system of Small Firms Bureaux. When the Government acted on the recommendations in 1973, the SED agreed to allow three of its remaining CIs (Robert Gordon's Institute of Technology in Aberdeen, and Dundee and Paisley Colleges of Technology) to retain their ILO posts if they wished to do so, but only within their academic staff complements.

Principal Howie, who, as Head of the Department of Civil Engineering, had been involved in testing work for the construction industry and related research at the beginning of the College's consultancy role, was committed

John Wylie MBE.

to the Industrial Liaison Service. In order to maintain the contact and goodwill already established with industry and commerce, and to avoid losing spin-off opportunities for consultancy and research work, the College absorbed the ILO post within its academic complement.

In 1973, therefore, the Industrial Liaison Service within Paisley College of Technology was reformed into the Centre for Liaison with Industry and Commerce (CLIC). 'We actually coined that word before Jimmy Saville thought of the safety-belt slogan,' John Wylie points out.

CLIC's creation freed the College from constraints formerly laid down by the Ministry of Technology and the Department of Trade & Industry. An Industrial Register and other data sources were set up, backed by market research to identify industrial and other needs. Visits to firms continued, and assistance was given on sandwich course placements, by then integral to most of the College's degree courses.

During the late 1960s and early 1970s, there had been a significant surge in industrial demand for short courses on pneumatics and hydraulics (the Low Cost Automation Centre). This continued to be built up, and in the 1970s many of CLIC's activities centred on the provision of short courses, with CLIC personnel providing input to course planning and occasional teaching on aspects of industrial organisation and management.

Conferences were also promoted. The first to be held on an international scale was the Tribology Conference in 1969 (again, a Ministry of Technology/Department of Trade & Industry initiative.) Tribology is the science of lubrication, friction and wear. These conferences, which involved a Scots night and a dinner as well as substantial technical content, were the precursors of the later, equally successful, Composite Structures conferences.

SSNDT

A major move in the development of links with industry came in 1974, with the establishment of the Scottish School of Non-Destructive Testing (SSNDT).

During the 1960s, the Department of Mechanical and Production Engineering's special expertise in welding had resulted in a series of short courses for industry. 'Willie McEwan, who had already been providing ultrasonic testing training courses, saw an opportunity for Paisley in the development of the offshore North Sea oil industry,' says John Wylie.

After talking to the Manpower Services Commission (MSC) and the Scottish Office, Willie McEwan, Harry Adams and others put together a proposal to set up a centre at Paisley College of Technology, for the purpose of training in ultrasonics and other methods of non-destructive testing for the offshore industry.

By the end of the decade, the School, set up in Westerfield House in

SSNDT students underwater weld testing at Fort William.

The opening of MIQAL, the Microelectronics and Quality Assurance Laboratory. In the left foreground are: Professor Lionel Davis, Scottish Office Minister Allan Stewart and Lecturer Alan Watt. Pictured in the doorway is Vice-Principal Downie.

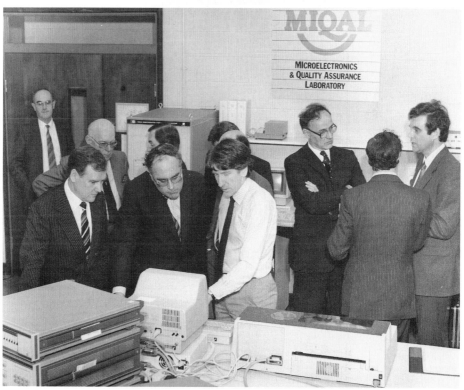

Tom Farmer opens the Quality Centre in 1990.

The Technology and Business Centre (completed 1986) was financed by the college and local business and provided a purpose-built venue for industrial seminars and courses.

SSNDT weld testing at Westerfield.

1974 and later moved to G Block, the original George Street building, had become the only external centre in the UK for the testing and certification of welding inspectors, and, like MACDATA, was attracting major research sponsorship.

Quality Centre

Professor William McEwan OBE.

The Quality Centre 'grew,' explains Professor William McEwan, OBE, 'out of a diversifying range of activities in the 1980s, and a changing emphasis in business. As a starting point, the Training Agency awarded £24,000 for a survey on the quality needs of the offshore industry. From that survey, it was apparent that industry was looking for undergraduate programmes in quality Management and Technology, rather than Quality Management alone.' SSNDT was brought together with MIQAL (Microelectronics Quality Assurance Laboratory) to form the Quality Centre. Programmed courses were run, together with joint courses for companies such as Babcocks. The first post-graduate programme of its kind in Scotland, the Post-graduate Diploma in Quality Engineering, was set up in 1977. The Quality Centre now covers virtually every spectrum, including engineering, leisure, tourism, health care, art, banking, public and social services.

MEDC

The growing interest in microprocessor technology had caused Peter Williams and Jack Carruthers of the Electrical Department to begin running courses in the 1970s, with CLIC involved in their marketing, selling and organisation. As microprocessors became more important, Peter Williams, who identified the opportunity to develop an industrial unit, put together a proposal, with Principal Howie's support.

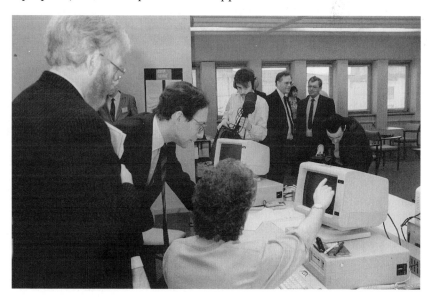

Peter Williams and Scottish Secretary Malcolm Rifkind pictured at the opening of MEDC in 1985.

MEDC building in Storie Street.

Experience gained through the MACDATA and SSNDT Special Units, combined with the College's central location and growing expertise in micro-electronics, resulted in a Scottish Office/SED decision to house Scotland's training centre for the electronics industry – the Microelectronics Educational Development Centre (MEDC) – on campus.

Although managed by the College, the centre was not part of it, and was not represented in the Senate or the Academic Board or within the faculties. It is funded by the Scottish Office until 1998, when funding will be taken over by those further education Colleges making use of its facilities.

David Jenkins was instrumental in helping the College to establish a Microsystems Centre on-campus – another DTI initiative – in the 1970s.

CLIC played a large part in all those initiatives. John Wylie viewed his role as that of '. . . a catalyst, very crucially dependent on the ideas of people like Willie McEwan, Peter Williams, and David Jenkins.' As he saw it, the creation of each new unit relied first on the entrepreneur with the ideas and the dynamics, secondly on the endorsement and support of the Principal, the Board of Governors, and John Oswald, as College Secretary, and, finally, on CLIC and its network of contacts.

Access to Technology

A growing interest in small business start-ups early in the 1980s meant that CLIC had become involved in the setting-up of a Small Business Unit, with help from the Economics and Management Department, and a part-time secondment. By the end of the 1980s, CLIC was running the Small Business Centre, the Industrial Liaison Centre, and the Access to Technology project (funded by the European Regional Development Fund).

Linwood and the Rover Group

In an effort to keep courses in step with changing technology, specialist options were developed, subject to factors such as staff availability. In this way, the College's engineering courses were among the first in Scotland to incorporate Computer Assisted Design/Computer Assisted Manufacture (CAD/CAM) technology. This had a number of important spin-offs, among them a significant collaboration with the Rover group of car manufacturers.

In 1981 a body-blow had been dealt to the Paisley area when the Peugeot car-manufacturing plant in Linwood, formerly the Rootes plant, closed down. At one time 8,000 people had been employed there, but the numbers had been whittled down to approximately 2,000 by the time it closed. By then there was little scope for re-employment in the area, and the knock-on effect was heavy.

Before the factory's closure, its welding manager had worked closely with the College on a number of projects. He later became an executive manager with the Rover Group, and through his earlier contact, Rover turned to the College for assistance when they were redesigning and developing their manufacturing processes in the mid-80s.

The result was a three-year partnership between Paisley College of Technology and the Rover Group, as they developed their manual-type approach with semi-automation into a fully-automated robotic approach to the development of chassis in Landrover vehicles. A large Landrover chassis was worked on for many years on-campus, and Rover incorporated some of the College's ideas into their new technology.

Links have been maintained ever since; in 1995 a Rover Group team visited the College to give a presentation to 220 final-year school pupils on the subject of new technology and engineering.

Industrial Engineering Students

Local history was made in 1982, when the College's first Industrial Engineering students graduated. Among their number was a 24 year-old Iranian, Afsaneh Mahmoodian, the first female to take the course. She and her fiancee, Davood Sarchamy, joined the course together, and graduated on the same day. They then opted for a further two years' study in the CAD/CAM Centre because, said Afsaneh, 'We both wanted to continue our studies, and Paisley College of Technology has the best system in the country.' The couple later married, and took up employment with BAe's Airbus project.

Expanding Horizons

In 1978 Tom Howie, who had an established reputation throughout the UK in the field of education and training, particularly of civil engineers, was invited to join a World Bank team as a consultant. The team was detailed to look at engineering education in Nepal, to help decide if that country should be given World Bank funding to improve its facilities and bring teaching methods and curriculum to a higher standard.

Finance was approved, subject to a technical and supervisory input from a developed country. The United Kingdom offered to finance this element, and Tom Howie was invited to submit proposals, as the most immediate requirement was to raise the standards in Civil Engineering, which were currently at 'trades' level and needed to be raised to diploma and, hopefully, degree level.

The Overseas Development Agency (ODA) eventually awarded a contract to Paisley College of Technology, whose proposals were unusual in that they involved groups of 3-4 specialists spending periods of time in Nepal, rather than 1-2 persons going there on a full-time basis. Once a specialist had been to Nepal and helped his Nepalese colleague to write course material, identify equipment needs, etc., the Nepalese would visit Paisley for several weeks to see how the courses were presented here.

'Right, who would like to go to Kathmandu?'

When Tom Howie said these words to a staff meeting in November 1977, 'There was a stunned silence,' recalls John Paul, a lecturer in Civil Engineering from 1963-1990. Once they had recovered from the shock, about half the department volunteered for the trip.

Tom Howie was the project Director, and Sam Leith, Senior Lecturer in Civil Engineering, took over the task of Project Co-ordinator, dividing his time between Paisley and Nepal. The administrative end of the contract was handled in Paisley by the College administration staff.

The first group left Paisley in April 1978. A villa (known to some locals as "The Scottish Embassy") was rented in a suburb of Kathmandu for the visiting specialists, who travelled by Land Rover between it and the Institute of Engineering at the Tribhovan University. The British Council, which had made all the arrangements in Kathmandu, was their postal address. 'The Council may not have been particularly happy with all those Scots descending on them,' John Paul reflected years later.

Over the next 4/5 years, the villa was in constant use as various specialists' inputs were made to the project. As the job developed, the important co-ordination role became a full-time job, and Jim Stoddart, a Senior Lecturer in the Civil Engineering Department, was seconded on a full-time basis to the project. He and his wife took up residence in Nepal for the rest of the project's duration.

Chemist James Cunningham Jack, author of *The College Poems 1939-1989*, recorded a poignant moment when he and his group celebrated St Andrew's Night in Nepal with Scottish meat sandwiches prepared by their local cook from a smuggled haggis.

The University of Tribhovan.

Fair fa' your honest triangular face
Great chieftain o' the sandwich-race
Aboon them a', ye tak' your place,
Fish, ham and egg.
Weel are ye worthy o' a grace
As lang's my leg!

The Nepalese College consisted of an old palace with a number of peripheral buildings. Paisley's remit was to design buildings and laboratories, specify equipment, design syllabuses for the courses, and check the equipment when it was installed.

About two years into the project, Tom Howie was asked to look at the possibility of creating a "trades" college at Dhahran in Eastern Nepal. The College was contracted by the ODA to supervise this work as well. The bulk of the required technical input was supplied by various further education colleges in Strathclyde Region, and by Jordanhill College of Education.

The Project's driver in Nepal.

Nepalese staff of the 'Paisley' House.

Within Paisley College of Technology, the projects, initially confined to the Civil Engineering Department, drew in staff members from some other departments as they proceeded. Lecturers from the Nepalese College as well as from its teacher-training College were involved in the teaching side of the project, while Paisley taught lab work. Paisley College of Technology was compensated for the use of its staff by the Overseas Development Agency.

All in all, the College was involved in Nepal until the mid-1980s, and what came to be called "The Nepal Project" left the participants with warm memories. The nature of the projects called for such close interaction between the Nepalese and the Scots that it is said that on one occasion, when a Paisley College staff member enquired in Delhi Airport about the next plane to Kathmandu, the official behind the desk remarked, 'You must come from Paisley.'

When John Paul retired in 1990, he and his wife visited Nepal, where they received a warm welcome. 'Everywhere we went, I was introduced as "a man from Paisley."'

The Paisley Conferences

In 1980, lecturer Ian Marshall, later to become Head of the Department of Mechanical and Manufacturing Engineering, decided that Paisley College of Technology should host a conference on composite structures (materials made up of two or more parts, the most common being fibre glass combined with other materials).

'Composite structures was a new area, and until then there had been no world-wide conference on the subject. I spoke to College Secretary John Oswald, about it, and he, being a pragmatist, said, "Yes, Ian, we're quite happy to give you the finance to start this conference, but if it fails you will be running short courses for the College for many years to make up the deficit."'

The first conference was held in 1981, modelled on the Tribology

Surplus money from the Nepal Project went into a Trust Fund, some of which was used to refurbish the Fisherman's Hut in Craigtoun Park, St. Andrews which had been used for many years by Paisley Civil Engineering students on field trips. The picture shows Paisley lecturers John G. Paul (left) J.H. Clark (3rd left) J. D. Younger (4th left) and Dr J. Lawson (5th left) with North East Fife Council staff and the team who carried out the work.

Professor Ian H. Marshall

conferences, and thanks to careful advance planning on Professor Marshall's part, plus strong support from his colleagues, it was a success. One hundred and twenty people from some 20 countries attended, the conference proceedings were published, and before it ended a second conference was proposed, to be held two years later.

The Paisley Conferences, as they are known worldwide, have been held on a regular two-year basis ever since. The 'proceedings volumes' brought out after each conference have a wide international circulation in technical universities and large companies, and in the early 1980s the international journal of Composite Structures was launched, with Professor Marshall as editor-in-chief, a position he still holds.

New Buildings

As a result of the Secretary of State's ruling, in 1968, that the College should remain in Paisley, plans were made for the development of the site. Phase One of the plan – the Civil and Mechanical Engineering Departments – was opened in 1973, and named the Henry Building in honour of former Principal, Hugh Henry.

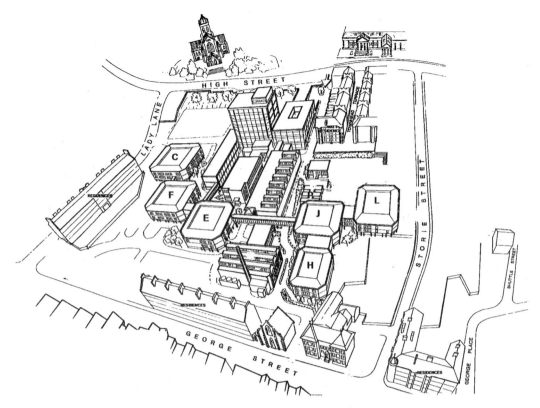

The College Buildings in the 1970s

Between 1970 and 1980 six structurally identical system-built blocks were added to the existing buildings. These were 'F', 'E' and 'J' (1973), 'H' (1974), 'L' (1976) and 'C' (1980) designed by Robert Matthew Johnson-Marshall and Partners. For a time, the increased accommodation almost eliminated the use of local church halls as lecture rooms, although a further increase in numbers in the late 1970s meant that lectures were again held in off-campus halls.

The Buildings planned in Principal Kerr's time but completed in the 1980s included H and J and L Block collectively known as the Elles Building.

The opening of the Denholm Building in 1980. Left to Right: James Denholm, Principal Howie, George Younger (Secretary of State) and Mrs Denholm.

The Underwood Residence opened in 1982.

Robin Elles had retired as Chairman of the Board of Governors in 1974. The Elles Building, which was formally opened in the same year, acknowledged his considerable contribution to the growth of the College during his time as a Governor. This Phase Two building consisted of the Library and the Departments of Social Studies, Mathematics, and Electrical Engineering.

The Denholm Building, the third and final phase of the expansion planned in 1967/68, was opened in 1980 by George Younger, then Scottish Secretary of State. The inauguration of the new building, which housed the Biology and Physics Departments, gave satisfaction to the many lecturers and former students who had expressed their eagerness in the past to see John Denholm, father of Vice-Principal James Denholm, properly honoured for the sterling work he had done for the College.

Even with the Denholm Building in use, and the College mainly housed in modern purpose-designed accommodation, more space was required, and Westerfield and other temporary accommodation had to be retained for teaching purposes.

The continuing problem of accommodation for students eased when some space was obtained at Craigie College in Ayr and Hamilton College of Education, both teacher-training Colleges, and both suffering a reduction in student numbers. The use of the residences, however, involved a considerable amount of travelling for students.

There was still a need, too, for social and communal accommodation, with about 40% of the students requiring housing as near to the College as possible. In 1980, work began on a purpose-built residence for 170 students on the north side of Oakshaw, and additional accommodation for a further 120 students was eventually made available through the acquisition of property in George Street and Lady Lane. Other flats throughout the town were leased from the local authority. Paisley College of Technology was probably the first College to house students in local authority rented accommodation .

Agreement was reached with the SED for additional building to meet a revised target of 3,000 full-time students – the figure predicted by Dr Kerr some ten years earlier. Diversification beyond the original core of Science and Engineering meant that by the 1980s, there were 10 academic departments within three Schools or Faculties, as compared to five departments in 1965.

Thornly Park Student Village

An Industrial School had been built in 1910 at Thornly Park, on the outskirts of Paisley, to house juvenile delinquents and truants. In 1975, a fire badly damaged the school, then classed as a List D institution, and in 1980 it was closed down.

When the 27-acre site went up for sale, it was considered to be ideal for the College. Apart from accommodation for some 300 students, the site included a sports hall and playing fields, facilities that the College had lacked for many years. The SED agreed to provide funds for the purchase, but at that time it was not possible for the College to borrow the money needed to bring the site up to standard. In the meantime, some students were housed in existing Thornly Park staff housing, and the sports hall was put into use, although in general the facilities were poor.

It was 1992 before it was possible to borrow the necessary funds for the Thornly Park renovations, and then only with Scottish Office permission. The College authorities grasped the opportunity, and some four and a half million pounds went into turning the Thornly Park campus into a students' village, with major financial assistance from the Robertson Trust.

Computer Developments

The second major period in the life of the Computer Centre began in the summer of 1974, with the installation of a Burroughs B5700 computer, a Twin Processor with 32K memory, card reader, line printer, two magnetic tape units, a fixed disk, ten VDU terminals, and four teletype terminals.

Its installation meant that data preparation was transferred from paper tape to punched cards. IBM card punches were purchased, and some of the teletypes originally used for paper tape preparation were used as terminals. 'The B5700 was a second-hand machine originally costing approximately £500,000,' Alan Wilson recalls, 'which was obtained for just over £100,000. The processor was such an enormous beast that we couldn't find a room large enough to accommodate the whole machine and the card reader and line printer had to be installed in a separate, adjacent room.' Two rooms in F block housed the Burroughs system.

'As the new machine was capable of handling both batch-processing and time-sharing simultaneously, users and applications were transferred from the 1901 and the PDP-8/E to the B5700 during 1974/75. In 1975, the 1901 was given to the Scottish College of Textiles at Galashiels, where computing requirements were not developing as rapidly as at Paisley, and the PDP-8/E was transferred to the Civil Engineering Department. Also, in 1975, at the request of the SED, we installed Post Office Datel equipment to provide a computing service to several further education colleges within

Prime Computer
and Operators in
'H' Block c. 1979.

Strathclyde Region. The colleges dialled into the B5700 in the same way as we had previously accessed the commercial time-sharing bureaux.

'We were soon to learn, to our cost, that the "bargain" we had purchased did not perform as we had expected. It became necessary to separate batch-processing jobs from time-sharing usage due to slow response times. The B5700 was frequently unreliable, with numerous "system hangs", much to the frustration of our users. Unfortunately, we had an obsolete machine and Burroughs were short of support staff knowledge on the B5700. Consequently, the service we received left much to be desired.

'The VDUs, which were Burroughs' own brand, often caused the system to crash, adding to our problems. Eventually, Burroughs reluctantly removed them, and refunded their total original cost. We then purchased more reliable replacement VDUs from another source. After two full academic sessions, and a large number of dissatisfied users, the Computer Facilities Committee investigated the market for alternative, up-to-date time-sharing systems. The B5700 was to remain in the College until 1979, only servicing the administration systems in batch mode in its latter days, before it was eventually scrapped. No tears were shed!

'Following the unfortunate experience of the B5700, a thorough investigation of available computer systems took place over a six-month period commencing summer 1976. The aim was to install a machine to provide a satisfactory time-sharing service, leaving the B5700 to cope with the larger batch jobs for which it was better suited.

'Eventually, a relatively small prime P300 computer was installed in the newly-built H Block in early 1977. It provided a service for 32 simultaneous users, based on a processor with a 128K memory and a 60 M disk, for the remainder of the 1976-77 session. The system was extremely reliable and popular with users, and it soon became necessary to upgrade it. The P300 processor was replaced by a faster P400 to service 48 terminal users for the start of the 1977-78 session.

'On the staffing side, a major reorganisation of the former Computer Unit was carried out in 1978. Ian Miller and Olav Marjasoo transferred from the Mathematics and Computing Department to join Alan Wilson, the previous Computer Unit manager. The Computer Centre was created with Ian Miller as Director, plus several more system and applications programmers resulting in a staff of twenty-four.'

75th Anniversary

In 1976 the College's 75th anniversary (again based on 1900/1901 as the commencement) was celebrated with a service in Paisley Abbey, conducted by the Abbey minister and the Rev. Robert Morrison of Orr Square Church, a representative of the Brough Trust and the longest-serving College Governor. A civic reception was held in Paisley Central Library.

Graduation ceremonies continued to be held in Paisley Town Hall during the 1980s, with officials and graduates walking through the town afterwards, on their way back to the College buildings.

Governors

The Rev. Robert Morrison

In the 1986 ceremony, an Honorary Fellowship was awarded to the Rev. Robert Morrison, minister of Orr Square Church for 38 years and Convenor of the Student Affairs Committee from the late 1950s. Conferring the honour, Principal Howie said, 'Our Fellowships are not awarded lightly, and are made to individuals whose contribution has been of the highest order.'

Interviewed after receiving the Fellowship, Mr Morrison recalled how he used to be able to see the College from his church. 'Now,' he said with wry humour, 'the College has grown so much that I can barely see anything else.'

From Student to Governor

In 1976, two former students became College Governors. Dr Johnston F. Robb, the student who had, with James Denholm's assistance, returned to Paisley from Newcastle in 1947 in order to complete his Engineering BSc, had become a director of Scott's Shipbuilding Company. A considerable number of Scott's employees studied at the College, and Principal Howie invited Dr Robb to join the Board.

Stuart Emery had become Managing Director of Clifton & Baird of Johnstone (he and his family later bought the company) and was deeply involved in the Paisley and Johnstone Training Group. 'Johnstone was the area for machine tools because of the local textile industry,' he explained in a 1996 interview. 'The machine tools industry developed from the textile industry's need of machinery. Eventually, textiles declined, but the machine tool industry grew.'

The Paisley and Johnstone Training Group were instrumental in the building of a Training Centre

The Reverend Robert Morrison, Minister of Orr Square Church, Paisley, the representative of the Brough Trustees on the Board of Governors over four decades.

Stuart Emery MBE.

in Johnstone, near Clifton & Baird's factory, training groups of up to 120 apprentices, with a coursework link-up with Paisley's Reid Kerr College.

Through his work with the Training Centre, Mr Emery became a prominent member of the Employers' Association, which nominated him onto Paisley College of Technology's Board of Governors. Governors were given a choice of committees to sit on, covering Students, Finance or Buildings. Stuart Emery opted for the Buildings Committee, having developed a knowledge of buildings through his work with the Training Centre. Fire safety and the provision of non-smoking areas was a concern to this committee. At that time the Building Committee Convenor was Sir James MacFarlane, who, said Mr Emery, 'smoked like a chimney. Tom Howie had to be diplomatic with him.'

Stuart Emery eventually became Convenor of the Buildings Committee and, later, chairman of the Board of Governors.

Merger Proposal

In 1978, Paisley College of Technology and the University of Stirling had discussed, informally, a possible union. The discussions had ended following a change of Principal at Stirling but in 1982 when Paisley was threatened with the loss of two important departments, they were resumed. Working titles of Wallace University and the New University of Scotland were considered, but once again, the talks ended, this time because Paisley's Board of Governors was not convinced of the value of the project.

By the 1980s the College had, as best it could within the limits of its resources, developed a range of services appropriate to an institution of higher education. Its academic staff was comparable in quality and experience with similar institutions, and it had consistently followed a policy of educational development designed to establish it as a university-level institution.

Principal Tom Howie

Principal Howie's sudden death in 1986 came as a severe blow to the staff and everyone associated with Paisley College of Technology. Most of his adult life had been spent there, as a student, lecturer, Head of the Department of Civil Engineering, Vice-Principal then Principal, presiding over times of change and expansion, yet managing at all times to retain the College's family image and caring nature.

'Tom became Principal just when the new buildings had arrived and the College was in need of consolidation,' said John Oswald. 'That's what he gave it. He was a first-class teacher and a real gentleman, and was very involved with the CNAA. The Nepal project came to Paisley purely because of Tom's contacts.'

John Paul, who worked with Tom Howie in the Civil Engineering Department, says, 'Tom Howie was an absolute gem . . . a real gentleman and a superb Head of Department', while Professor John Smyth recalls Principal Howie as a 'friendly, approachable personality', a view echoed by staff and students alike.

Principal Howie at a Graduation in Paisley Town Hall in the 1980s.

Chapter 8
Principal Richard Shaw
(1986-)

Richard Shaw, Head of the Department of Economics and Management, had only been Vice-Principal for a matter of weeks when Tom Howie's sudden death thrust him into the post of Acting-Principal.

Principal Shaw.

A native of Preston, he gained his BA Honours degree at Cambridge and lectured in Economics in the Universities of Leeds and Stirling and, as a visiting lecturer, in the University of Newcastle, New South Wales, Australia, before coming to Paisley in 1984. In 1987 he was officially appointed as the new Principal of Paisley College.

He took up the post at a time of change within tertiary education. Because of this, a major part of his remit involved taking a new, strategic look at the direction in which the College was going, and where the students were coming from. He has also had to take on the challenging task of expanding the horizons, looking at diversification into different areas, and seizing opportunities which have evolved in terms of different courses and different student mixes.

The main developments have been the granting of University status, the doubling of student numbers through expansion and mergers, and the introduction of innovative types of courses.

Towards a University of Paisley

During the late 1980s, the College took a major step towards independence and academic maturity when it was granted accredited status, giving it the right to conduct its own course approval events without having to refer back to the CNAA. In 1990 it was one of only a few institutions granted the authority by the CNAA to confer awards on the Council's behalf, in recognition of its academic integrity and stringent quality procedures.

A White Paper published in 1991 made it possible for polytechnics (the English equivalent of Central Institutions) to gain university status if they so wished, but unfortunately, the situation was not so simple for Scottish institutions.

The College already had the necessary CNAA accreditation, was highly degree-orientated, and had a good reputation, with its graduates valued in many industries. Since the 1950s it had forged strong links with industry, and now it turned to its industrial friends for assistance.

'With the personal support of the Chief Executives of many large firms, and with the help of our own Governors, we managed to press for a meeting with Michael Forsyth, then Scottish Minister for Education,' said Principal Shaw. 'It was a very nervous time for us.'

Ian Lang, Secretary of State for Scotland at the time, gave his backing to university status at the end of 1991, but student numbers still posed a problem. Higher Education institutions seeking university status were required to have 4,000 full-time equivalent students on degree level work, a figure which Paisley had not yet achieved . As the students' newsletter of the time put it; 'Question – What's the difference between a College and a University? Answer – About 2,000 students.'

Even when the required figure was reached, the nail-biting continued. The legislation had to go through Parliament, and because of a forthcoming General Election, Parliamentary time almost ran out. But the legislation scraped through, and in April 1992, on the day before Parliament broke up for the elections, the Queen signed the papers, and Paisley College became one of the 'new' universities.

'It was so close!' Principal Shaw recalls.

From the summer of 1992, the College had the right to call itself the University of Paisley, though the new title still had to be approved by the Privy Council. Letters of support were obtained from Renfrew District Council, Renfrewshire Enterprise, Paisley Chamber of Commerce, and Glasgow and Strathclyde Universities.

Arthur Hughes, a College technician between 1957-1987, said proudly in a recent interview, 'I immediately told my friends that I merited more respect, for I was no longer a retired college technician – I was a retired university technician!'

Coats Memorial Graduations

In 1992 a new venue was found for graduations – the Thomas Coats Memorial Baptist Church, directly opposite the University. Built by the family that donated the original George Street site for the proposed Technical School and supported it with further donations over the years, the church is one of Paisley's architectural jewels. Its great stone staircase, sweeping down to the High Street, provides a superb setting for graduates and academic staff in their ceremonial robes on Graduation Days. The church is also the University's chaplaincy centre, and its lower halls are used for lecture purposes.

Sir Robert Easton

In June 1993 Sir Robert Easton, Chairman of Yarrow Shipbuilders on the Clyde and a Scottish industrialist of high standing, was formally installed as the first Chancellor of the University of Paisley at a colourful ceremony in Coats Memorial Church.

Sir Robert, who had received an Honorary Fellowship from the University in 1992 in recognition of his services to industry, was also the first to be awarded the degree of Doctor of the University of Paisley (DUniv).

Academic Dress

University Bedellus Douglas Bell with ceremonial robes and mace.

To mark the move in status from College to University, the former Academic Board was renamed the Senate, and a new set of academic dress and regalia was commissioned. After researching old Paisley patterns, Scotland's last handloom linen weaver produced a design reflecting the University's home town, its industrial heritage and its origins in the School of Art/Design.

Featuring the famous pine motif inset with smaller pines, representing growth and regeneration and the University's development, the pattern, woven into red damask brocade, is featured on undergraduate, postgraduate and honorary degree hoods and gowns.

The Universities of Glasgow and Strathclyde generously gifted robes, bearing the new design, for the Chancellor and Vice-Chancellor.

The Enlargement of the New University

An increase in student numbers was one of the criteria for the granting of University status, and Paisley gained from a natural rise in the numbers of people entering higher education at this time. However, a significant number of new students came from mergers and affiliations with other colleges – in particular, Craigie College of Education in Ayrshire, and the awarding of a contract for the provision of education for nurses by the Health Boards of Argyll and Clyde, and Ayrshire and Arran.

Craigie College

At a press conference in March 1992, just weeks before university status was finally achieved, Principal Shaw and Principal Gordon Wilson of Craigie College in Ayrshire announced a merger between their two Colleges under the name (it was then hoped) of the University of Paisley, with Craigie as the Faculty of Education.

Gordon Wilson. Principal of Craigie College at the time of the merger, now Assistant Principal of the University.

Craigie College of Education opened in 1964 as an all-female college, training primary education teachers. Eventually it began to take male students as well, but by 1976/77 the demand for extra primary teachers had dropped to such an extent that Craigie was threatened with closure. Throughout the years it had enjoyed an excellent professional reputation, and on this occasion a vigorous campaign won a reprieve. In 1986, however, it again came under threat.

Located in the former Craigie Estate, Ayr, the College has a fine campus boasting an eighteenth century mansion house, halls of residence, ample playing fields and superb educational and professional facilities.

The merger with the University of Paisley, achieved in 1993, has been of considerable benefit to both institutions. As well as combining the study of technology and education, it has made Paisley a two-campus university and has given new purpose to Craigie, which had only 500 students at the time of the merger. By the autumn of 1995, Craigie had already become a multi-disciplinary campus with over 1,200 students. By a happy coincidence, the Scottish Office letter giving official approval to the merger between the University and College arrived on the day of Paisley's first graduation ceremony as a University, and in April 1993 the University Constitution came into force.

The first students arrive in uniform to enrol at Craigie College in 1964.

A visit by the Secretary of State to Craigie College c. 1972. On the left of the picture Craigie staff include Mr Keegan, Mr Drummond, Mrs Smith and Mrs Rennie who was Principal at the time of the visit. Also pictured is Ayr MP George Younger.

Craigie House, 18th Century mansion scheduled to open in late 1997 as Ayr Management Centre.

Associated Colleges

In 1994 the University awarded associate status to Greenock's James Watt College of Further and Higher Education, the Reid Kerr College in Paisley, and Ayr and Kilmarnock Colleges, giving their students, together with students in some other further education centres, the opportunity, if they wish, to use their Higher National Diplomas as a stepping stone, and go on to achieve degrees from the University of Paisley.

Under the associateship scheme, Paisley develops a programme equivalent to its own first-year courses, which the Colleges are licensed to use. Once students complete these courses they can, if they so wish, continue their studies in the University without having to repeat any work.

'It's part of a sea-change,' explains Principal Shaw. 'We all used to be islands – secondary schools didn't communicate with primary schools, colleges didn't communicate with secondary schools, universities didn't communicate with colleges. Now we're all communicating and working together. Our Heads of Departments are also in personal contact with Departmental Heads in various further education colleges. This is all about widening educational opportunities for students who want to move on and gain more qualifications.'

CATS

One of the principal ways in which Paisley has widened opportunities and increased student numbers is the innovative Credit Accumulation and Transfer Scheme (CATS).

Attending a conference in Jordanhill College of Education in Glasgow in the late 1980s, Principal Shaw, John Wylie and Professor Philip Bunn, then Head of the Electrical Engineering Department, were introduced to the scheme. It is an education programme which allows flexibility and choice to students, both in terms of qualification sought and the subjects studied.

CATS gives students the freedom to follow individual study programmes catering for their own interests and needs, by subdividing courses into units, each unit having an associated number of CATS credit points. This enables the student to negotiate a study programme that may, in some cases, include units gained at different institutions or through employers' training schemes.

Professor Alex MacLennan.

As each unit is successfully completed, its points are accumulated towards an eventual qualification.

The scheme interested Principal Shaw, who asked Professor Bunn to develop CATS at Paisley. The Technology and Business Centre, with its interest in continuing education, was also involved. Alex MacLennan then took over the successful development of the scheme, with John Wylie still involved via his role in development and enterprise, sponsorship and funding activities. In the early 1990s, British Petroleum subscribed £120,000 towards CATS from its 'Aiming for a College Education' scheme. Later, the Robertson

Trust donated £90,000. The College itself invested considerable funds to support the development of CATS.

Thanks to Philip Bunn's work in setting the project up, access to external funding which allowed expansion, and the drive and enthusiasm with which Alex MacLennan built the scheme up, CATS – generally agreed to be a major step forward in higher education – now plays a significant part in Paisley's education system.

Nursing Contract

The introduction of CATS opened the door to nursing courses in higher learning institutions. During Principal Howie's time the College began forging links with Argyll and Clyde Nursing College, and Richard Shaw continued the work when he became Principal. 'It was a case of small beginnings, but we worked hard at it,' he says. 'None more than Margaret McIntyre, a senior lecturer in the Department of Applied Social Studies.'

Nurses were keen to attend courses, and in time the links strengthened. With the development of nursing as a graduate profession Paisley was ready to take advantage of the new situation. During the 1990s hundreds of nurses in the West of Scotland have participated in Paisley's CATS scheme, many gaining degrees in health studies. Nurses were among the students at the 1995 graduation ceremony, and in 1996 the University won a five-year contract to provide nursing and midwifery education for the Argyll & Clyde and Ayrshire & Arran Health Boards, covering a large section of the West of Scotland from Oban to south Ayrshire. Education staff from the former nursing colleges, now members of the University staff, will play a key role in developing the new courses.

Other innovations in teaching methods include on-site courses and distance learning.

Distance Learning

Thanks to advances in communication and computer technology, students no longer have to travel to Paisley to become part of the University. In 1994 it launched its Distance Learning programme through On-line Education in Hong Kong, enabling students to study for an accredited UK award in their own homes with full tutor support. Each student is provided with an advanced personal computer and given training in the computer techniques necessary for studying and communication with the tutor. Students can also communicate with each other via computer teleconferencing.

The Paisley courses concentrate strongly on flexibility. In the MBA (Master of Business Administration) degree course, students can opt to take one, two or all three sections. The first section on its own gains the student a Certificate in Business Development, the second a Diploma in Management Studies, and those who take and pass the full course graduate with a Master's degree in Business Administration.

Other Distance Learning courses are available at the time of writing in Quality Management and Computer Aided Engineering. Long distance graduates become members of the University of Paisley Alumni Association and can, if they wish, attend the graduation ceremony in Paisley, although there have been graduations in Shetland and Dumfries.

As Principal Shaw sees it, 'We in Paisley are here to provide a service. The British way has always included small-group teaching and personal contacts between staff and students. The cuts in Government education spending have made this increasingly difficult. In Paisley the students expect to know the staff and be able to turn to them for help when necessary, and the staff have always reciprocated. This important facility has been put at risk.

'Part of the answer might come from techniques developed in Distance Learning. Using Distance Learning materials and, possibly even lectures from places as far away as North America, students can be encouraged to study in their own way, at their own pace, and in their own time. By releasing some staff-time currently used for conventional teaching and preparation, it may be possible to enable staff to become more like educational consultants and counsellors.

'My personal vision is that we may end up with a form of active learning in which students take greater responsibility for their own education, with the staff providing guidance and help. In this way we would be making use of new technology to enhance higher education.

'Such a system would, of course, require a cultural change towards learning. It's not an easy path, but I believe that it's going to come. We're in the process of moving towards it. We have to be capable of using technology to our advantage.'

On-site Company Courses

Another innovative teaching method has been in place for a number of years. It takes the University to the students, with a policy of teaching employees on-site. For example, jointly-designed courses were developed for IBM at Greenock. With the help of IBM and local enterprise some of these courses have been adapted for other local firms. The Business Management degree is also being taught at the British Aerospace site in Prestwick.

Richard Shaw sees on-site learning as one of the ways in which the university can move forward. 'Flexibility is important – creating courses to suit various needs.'

This flexible approach, together with mergers and affiliations, brings over 6,000 students a year to Paisley, but despite the University's growth the caring element is still alive in the nineties. In former Secretary John Oswald's view, Paisley still has an emphasis on vocational education, an end product to the degree course. 'I think the traditional universities are moving closer to the Paisley ethic rather than the other way. Paisley almost has a cafeteria system, "Tell us what you want to study and we'll sort it out for you."'

To help in this process, Professor Alan Roach, Dean of Science, masterminded the development of the University's new modular structure while retaining a clear focus on vocational education.

Dr Frank Placido and the Scanning Electron Microscope in the Department of Physics.

The Department of Physics has several specialised laboratories – Laser, Glass Research, Nuclear Physics/Remote Sensing and the Clean Room, pictured here.

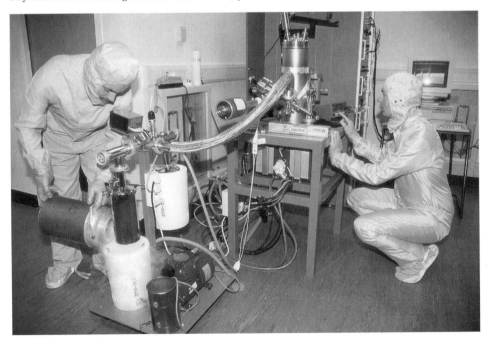

International Relations

Paisley's educational links with other countries, fostered by Principal Howie, continued and expanded under Principal Shaw.

Language Teaching

In the 1970s a suggestion that the College should incorporate language courses was rejected by the Scottish Office on the grounds that such courses were not sufficiently vocational. In the 1990s, however, language teaching was re-established, principally in the Department of Economics and Management. Professor Young takes up the story.

'This partly came about with the launch of the new BA Business and Management degree. A compulsory business French, business German, or business Spanish was built into the drafting of this degree (it was considered important for a modern manager to be familiar with one other language as well as English.)

'This led on to the desire to have staff members who could competently teach these languages, not in the traditional way, but as languages with a strong business orientation. It was soon realised that the very same arguments for a "language element" could be applied to other degree courses.'

These arguments were also, of course, in the context of moves, from the mid-80s onwards, to closer European integration. 'We felt that surely the time had come for us to ensure that British business-people are trained to function in the Euro market. We read up on various studies which indicated that while people in France or Germany might be willing to sell to us in English, they were more likely to buy from us in French or German. We tried to take this kind of thought on board.'

This meant increasingly trying to encourage students to find placements in France, Spain or Germany. John Struthers, then course leader for the Business Economics degree, was, says Professor Young, 'very active in this regard.'

Out of a review of courses in Business Economics taken around 1990/ 91 emerged Business Economics and European Economy with Languages. In 1995, around 40 students from France, Germany and Spain came into the department's third year classes.

There have been financial problems over increasing the number of such students, as the income generated from European Union students coming to Paisley is not substantial.

One possible area of expansion is to integrate more language teaching into other departments, a policy that could be used to attract students within the more expensive bands of student funding. 'Not just business economics with a language,' explains Professor Young, 'but computing or engineering with a language.' This may be a possible way to expand language teaching at Paisley, though a problem and an 'inhibitor' is that the proper teaching of languages is a labour-intensive activity, ideally done in relatively small groups. Vice-Principal Bill Stevely is particularly involved in links with the outside community.

The Soviet Connection

In 1989 the College had been startled by the unannounced and unexpected arrival of a high-ranking academician from Moscow's Soviet Academy of Science. The visitor, J. Fridlyander, had been sent to Paisley by the Minister of the Soviet Aviation Industry to attend the composites conference, apparently at the behest of then-President Gorbachev, because the Russians were eager to market scientific advances made in composite structures over the previous twenty-five years. The two-yearly Paisley Conference caused the Russians to decide on Paisley as their sole collaborating College.

Malcolm Rifkind, then Secretary of State for Scotland, and Professor Ian Marshall, Head of the Department of Mechanical and Manufacturing Engineering, visited Moscow where, in the Soviet Academy of Science, a Memorandum of Agreement was signed on behalf of the College and the Academy. In 1995 the results of the collaboration was published in six volumes.

A further connection with Russia arose after the break-up of the Soviet Union, when the University of Paisley assisted staff at Yaroslavl University to set up an International Business and Technology Centre.

The Far East and Egypt.

During the 1990s the Quality Centre has been acting as an independent advisor to the Department of Mines in Papua New Guinea, and a contact made in the 1970s with higher education in Egypt, via the Department of Mechanical Engineering and the SSNDT, led in 1995 to the creation of a new Institute of Productivity and Quality (modelled on the Paisley Quality Centre) at the Arab Academy for Science and Technology in Alexandria.

The Dean and Assistant Dean of the Egyptian Institute achieved their Doctorates at Paisley's Quality Centre, which is involved in running joint courses in Egypt. There has also been collaborative work between the Centre and the Institute with a view to establishing SCOTVEC programmes in Egypt.

Poland

In 1991 the University (then Paisley College) was awarded a £250,000 contract by the European Community to help Poland develop environmental protection facilities, including the setting-up of a specialist Government analytical laboratory in the Technical University of Radom. This built on a long-standing relationship with Radom, developed and nurtured over many years, primarily by Stuart Harvey, a senior lecturer in Chemistry.

Over a five-year period, Paisley oversaw the TEMPUS (Trans-European Mobility Programme for University Studies) project on environmental protection. Paisley was the lead institution collaborating with academic departments from Barcelona University in Spain and Dortmund University in Germany in the creation of an environmental laboratory and the training of Polish academics. Paisley's Centre for Environmental and Waste Management, which had only recently been set up, also contributed to the Polish programme. Dr Harry Rendall of the Department of Chemistry and

Professor McEwan signing the agreement with representatives of the Arab Academy for Science and Technology in Alexandria.

Professor McEwan at a meeting of the Taiwanese Students Association in the Brough Hall.

Principal Shaw, Chemistry and Chemical Engineering Dept. staff and representatives from the Universities of Radom, Barcelona and Dortmund on the occasion of the presentation of the K Pulaski Medal, 1992.

Chemical Engineering was project co-ordinator. In 1992 Paisley College of Technology was awarded the K. Pulaski Medal, Radom's highest honour.

In 1993 the International Relations Office was established to develop and reinforce Paisley's position in the international education market. Professor Philip Bunn, Head of the Department of Electrical and Electronic Engineering and Director of International Relations, emphasised the University's commitment as a key player in the international market for students.

During the 1990s, the University had seized every opportunity offered to expand and diversify, developing training in the caring professions, such as nursing and social work, as well as in engineering, science and technology, and business management. In addition to students on degree, diploma and postgraduate courses, an estimated 8,000 students attend short courses geared to enable them to study while in employment.

Student Life.
The Rent Strike

An attempt by the College authorities to increase rents during the 1990/91 student session, particularly for renovated housing in Lady Lane, met with protests from students, already hard hit by Government decisions to freeze grants, deny Income Support and Housing Benefit to students outwith term-time, and to limit the increase in student loans to only six percent.

A student march and demonstration during the rent strikes 1991/92.

When, despite objections, the Board of Governors voted for the rent increases, the students retaliated by calling for a rent-strike at the start of the 1991/92 session. The increase came at a time when U.K. students in general were angry over swingeing Government cuts in higher education, and the confrontation in Paisley attracted attention throughout the country. A Hardship Fund was set up in October 1990 and badges, mugs and T-shirts backing the students' views began to appear throughout the College. The fight was still raging at Christmas, with the students paying their rents and fees into a bank account set up by the Rent Strike Committee, instead of to the College.

The matter was finally settled when about 300 students marched through Paisley and occupied the Technology and Business Centre. Forty-eight hours later the Board of Governors and students' representatives agreed on a reasonable rent increase.

Nursery

A nursery was set up in Wallneuk North Church Hall in the late 1980s to cater for the children of students and staff members, and 1991 saw the completion of a five-year plan by the Students' Association to refurbish their Union, 'The B'roo', although at the time of writing the search continues for more spacious accommodation nearer, if not actually within, the main University campus.

Students' eye-view

'Getting to the Union can be difficult for students with mobility problems,' said Heather Watt, President of the Students' Association during 1995/96, 'though obviously it is difficult finding a suitable site right in the town.'

Heather found the University campus 'impressive, but claustrophobic', when she first arrived from Aberdeen. She became involved in student representation in her second year, and as President she sat on the University Court, the Senate, and all the Academic Boards. The Senior Vice-president, a student from Craigie campus, is also on the University Court. Part of Heather's remit was to bond the Paisley and Craigie students into a single two-campus university.

She found that financial hardship among students was one of the major problems encountered throughout her year in office. 'Grants have been cut, effectively, by 10 per cent in the past two years,' she said towards the end of the 1995/96 session, 'and students are ending their courses £4-5,000 in debt from student loans alone. A student cannot graduate if he or she is in debt to the University itself, and this year the Hardship Fund has been hit hard by students needing money to pay their rent so that they can go ahead and graduate.'

There are two Welfare Advisory Services, one run by the students, the other by the University; this enables students to choose between talking to other students or to University officials about their problems. Heather has found that, like the Hardship Fund, the Students' Welfare Service has been over-utilised, although accommodation problems have eased slightly. The George Street residence was refurbished in 1996, and the students' village at Thornly Park has proved to be a great success with those living there and/or using the sports facilities.

Heather, who studied in the Department of Social Studies, had nothing but praise for the lecturers she encountered. 'They were very approachable . . . well over half the students in Business and Social Studies are female though the Engineering Faculty is still male-dominated.'

One of the memories she has of being a Paisley student concerns the use of external halls for classrooms. One particular church hall in Shuttle Street (now demolished) had a leaky roof, and on rainy days Heather and her colleagues had to endure being dripped on from above.

Like Heather, Calum Coulter, an MSc student in Applied Social Studies 1990/95, found the College daunting when he first arrived, mainly because, in his view, new students were not given adequate guidance to help them locate the external annexes . 'I was well into my second year before I started frequenting the Students' Union,' says Calum, 'because it took me that length of time to actually find it . . . some students never find their way there. It's a pity it's so far from the campus.'

In his final year he himself acted as a guide to new students, and found it quite difficult explaining the somewhat rambling Paisley campus to newcomers. 'It's a good idea to use old church buildings for conservation purposes; most of them are very attractive on the outside and good acoustically, but some of the locations are obscure.'

Calum, who previously studied Civil Engineering at Glasgow University, found Paisley much more personalised, with students given every chance to get to know their lecturers and fellow-students. (He also considered the staff teaching methods to be far superior to anything experienced at Glasgow University. 'The lecturers at Paisley tend to be multi-tasking, and able to teach in various departments.')

New Courses, Centres and Units

The Craigie merger, CATS, and the nursing contracts brought many new subjects to the University. Health Studies, already part of Applied Social Studies, greatly expanded, as did language teaching in the Department of Economics and Management. Computer courses proliferated.

Professor Peter Bartos, Civil Engineering, was appointed as Personal Professor in recognition of his outstanding work in the field of Concrete and Cement research.

'One has only to compare the College Directory for 1986 with that of the University in 1996 to appreciate the enormous changes which have occurred over Professor Shaw's period of office to date' says Professor Roy Sinclair, formerly of the Department of Chemistry and Chemical Engineering and Chairman of the University Centenary Committee. 'Some of the main changes include the incorporation of Craigie College, a restructuring of the academic departments and faculty organisation, the reorganisation of the administrative structure and the creation of further industrial units, centres and support units. On the personnel side all the units have their Directors with technical and secretarial assistants, some of whom are concerned with the research, business and commercial aspects of the University and do not have a direct input to undergraduate teaching programmes. The appointment of personal Professors and Readers was instituted in 1988 to allow the University (along with external University assessors) to provide recognition for staff who had gained high reputations in their specialist fields, and/or in higher education activities. In addition a number of organisations have sponsored Professorial chairs including those in Enterprise & Development, Environmental Technologies and Health Studies. On the buildings side there has been continuous development at Craigie and Paisley supervised for over twenty years by Adam Lynch, Director of Estates and Buildings.'

Professor C M MacDonald, appointed Head of Department of Biological Sciences in 1992, a leading authority in genetic engineering.

Professor Reggie von Zugbach de Sugg. Now Head of Department of Management and Marketing was originally appointed as Personal Professor.

Expansion of Business Courses

In numerical terms, the Department of Economics and Management 'took off' in the late 1980s. There were eleven staff members in 1975, twenty-four in 1984, about thirty staff members by 1989, and sixty-one full-time members of staff by 1993. At the start of the 1995/96 session the department held a staff of more than seventy – about sixty-five full-time, and five or six part-time. At the end of 1996 it was divided into two departments.

'Over a period of maybe four years, we more than doubled in size from thirty to over sixty,' says Professor Young, 'A very rapid pace of expansion.' It is his view that the expansion of Economics and Management played an important part in the fight to gain university status.

In 1995, Glasgow's Mackintosh School of Architecture and Paisley University's Department of Civil Engineering combined to introduce architecture into the third year of Paisley's structural engineering degree course, thus giving the engineering students a feel for the aesthetics of building design.

Baptist College Courses

From September 1996 the Scottish Baptist College has been able to offer a new four-year BD course validated by the University of Paisley, the first of the new Scottish universities to award degrees in divinity. The Baptist College is affiliated to Craigie Faculty of Education, and divinity graduates will, aptly, be capped at University graduations in the Coats Memorial Baptist Church.

Educational Development Unit Courses

In 1971 William Craig, a Lecturer in the Department of Electrical Engineering had been appointed as full-time Director of Audio-Visual Aids, with a College-wide remit and a central role in staff development and training as well as in the preparation of teaching material. Eventually the Educational Development Unit (EDU) was created, with a full-time graphics and technical staff. Functioning as a department with its own budget, the new unit has greatly expanded the College's technical facilities. During the 1980s and 90s the Unit, under Director Bob Rowatt, developed the provision of courses for Staff Development and Media Studies.

Industrial Units Development

In December 1991 Scotland's new Metrology Centre, sited within the Department of Mechanical and Manufacturing Engineering, was opened by Mr Colin Smallwood, general manager of Rolls Royce plc in Hillington, who said that the new centre 'further enhanced Paisley's reputation as one of Scotland's top centres of engineering excellence.'

The Electro Magnetic Compatibility Centre, a service to industry led by F. Galbraith, has been set up by the University and local industry, and funding for the new Environmental and Waste Management Centre came from Scottish Enterprise and the industry.

In 1995 the Department of Trade & Industry chose Paisley University

William Craig pictured here on the right with the EDU staff of the late 1970s, when the Unit was presented with the Royal Television Society award for video production.

as the venue for their Scottish Support Centre programme, aimed at enabling smaller firms to make use of the latest developments in micro-circuitry. Microelectronics in Business (MIB) was set up within the Department of Electrical and Electronic Engineering, offering access to hardware, software, training and advice.

The Department of Land Economics has expanded its law teaching to a range of courses in other departments, mainly in business, construction and social studies. It also runs a Land Valuation Information Unit, a property databank based on information from the Register of Sasines in Edinburgh. Professor Will Fraser, Head of Land Economics, says, 'The Unit undertakes various research and consultancy projects, mainly for the surveying profession in the widest sense – in other words, the property profession or property market.' The databank, which also provides a subscription service to surveyors, estate agents, lawyers, building societies, etc., has approximately 300 clients, and is run as a commercial enterprise.

In conjunction with Scottish Enterprise, the department has also set up the Scottish Property Network, a databank part-funded by Strathclyde European Partnership.

Dr Andrew Hursthouse Director of the Centre for Particle Characterisation and Analysis, pictured here with students during an environmental project near Langbank.

The Strathclyde Integrated Development Operation and the European Regional Fund helped to establish the Centre for Particle Characterisation and Analysis in the Faculty of Science in 1993. It has at its disposal an array of analytical methods and equipment (including Chromatography, Spectroscopy and Microbiological analysis) which are used to assist small to medium size enterprises within the former Strathclyde Region.

Buildings

In 1994 the former George Street Baptist Church, altered into a 210-seat lecture hall, was named the Oswald Building in recognition of John Oswald, who had retired from the post of College Secretary in 1989. He received an Honorary Fellowship in 1991.

At the time of writing, work has commenced on a new Library Building and Learning Resource Centre with study space for more than 650 students as well as seminar and group study rooms. Efforts continue, throughout the university, to provide wider access to higher education for students with disabilities or special needs.

In May 1995 Thornly Park Sports Centre was officially opened by Craig Brown, manager of Scotland's football team and a former Craigie lecturer. Guests of Principal Shaw and members of the University Court present at the ceremony included William Barr, Chairman of Barr Construction (as well as being a former Paisley student, former Chairman of Craigie College of Education, and Chairman of Ayr United F.C.), and Mrs Howie, widow of former Principal Tom Howie, whose name was given to the sports hall within the Centre.

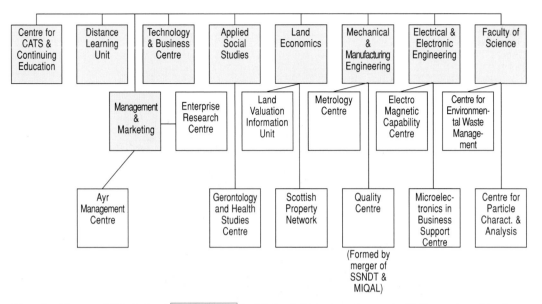

Centre for CATS & Continuing Education	Distance Learning Unit	Technology & Business Centre	Applied Social Studies	Land Economics	Mechanical & Manufacturing Engineering	Electrical & Electronic Engineering	Faculty of Science
		Management & Marketing	Enterprise Research Centre	Land Valuation Information Unit	Metrology Centre	Electro Magnetic Capability Centre	Centre for Environmental Waste Management
	Ayr Management Centre		Gerontology and Health Studies Centre	Scottish Property Network	Quality Centre	Microelectronics in Business Support Centre	Centre for Particle Charact. & Analysis

(Formed by merger of SSNDT & MIQAL)

Specialist Units in 1996. Related Departments highlighted. Units in existence in 1985 mentioned in the diagram on p 124 are not included (source: current internal directory).

Opening of EMC Centre . Scottish Industry Minister Allan Stewart MP (Centre) and his entourage are shown around the new EMC Centre at the University of Paisley by Director Farquhar Galbraith (right). Also in the picture are Dr George Bennett, corporate Vice President and General Manager of Motorola of East Kilbride, (to the Minister's right) and the company's Director of External Relations Mr Tony Joyce (extreme right).

The University's Economic Impact

A study by three members of the Department of Economics and Management into the impact made by the University of Paisley in the period 1993-95 shows that it had made a major economic and physical effect on the surrounding areas.

Direct expenditure by University staff and students was £44m in total in 1994, over £20m of which was spent directly in Renfrewshire and Ayrshire. Including multiplier effects, between £22m and £26m was generated in the Renfrewshire and Ayrshire economies, particularly in the areas of housing and services. Some £3.3m worth of contracts were awarded to local companies, particularly in building, maintenance and professional services.

The University is responsible for the creation of at least 3000 jobs across the country, about 1500 in Renfrewshire and 500 in Ayrshire, and some 100 students are placed in Renfrewshire companies and 50 each year in Ayrshire as an integral, paid part of their degrees, with many more in unpaid work placements in education, social work, and other programmes. Over 20% of students commence work in Renfrewshire or Ayrshire, and an estimated 25% eventually settle in employment locally.

Richard Shaw

Says Professor Roy Sinclair 'The caring reputation of staff at both Craigie and Paisley is one which Professor Shaw has been at considerable pains to maintain, despite all the staffing and financial pressures facing the University sector in the 1990s. Professor Shaw himself must be unique among Scottish University Vice-Chancellors in that he is known to virtually every member of staff of the University from the janitorial and cleaning staff to the Research Associates in some of our specialised units. As the University has expanded rapidly he has been supported in that approach by Assistant Principal Professor Gordon Wilson, the Vice-Principal and the University Secretary. To achieve personal recognition among a staff of over 1,200 people is remarkable, but Richard Shaw achieves that by personally attending as many special events within Departments, Divisions and Units as he can humanly manage (and sometimes at considerable personal inconvenience). The University is lucky to have a Vice-Chancellor at the helm who is widely respected internally but who is also highly regarded externally in higher education and business circles.'

Paisley Buildings

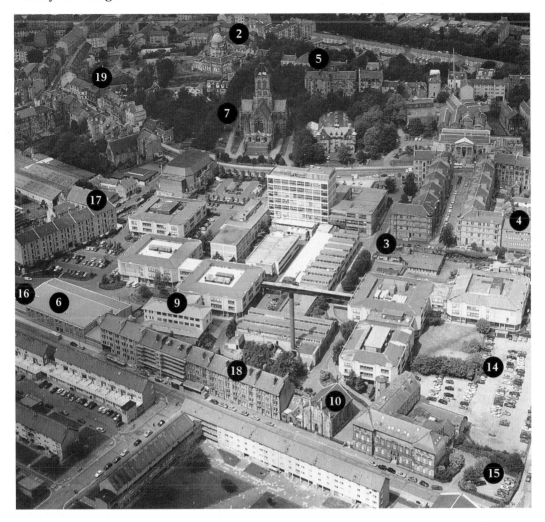

College / University Buildings 1980 to 1997

The area in central Paisley bounded by Lady Lane, High Street, Weighhouse Close and George Street was re-zoned for educational use in 1968 in the wake of the proposals to move to Erskine and the aborted public enquiry. In 1997, after over thirty years of negotiation, purchase and construction, almost all the property in the designated area belongs to the University. Of the post 1980 buildings, Frank Burnet Bell and Partners designed T.B.C., the Tom Howie Building, The Thornly Park Sports Centre and Student Village and the new Library and Learning Resources Centre.

The following properties within and beyond the designated area, were built, acquired or leased between 1980 and 1997.

1. Thornly Park purchase. Not shown (1980)
2. Underwood Residence
3. T.B.C. (1986)
4. MEDC (1988)
5. Disposal of 'Dunscore'. Acquisition of Harper Residence (1989)
6. Howie Building (1992)
7. Coats Memorial used for graduations (1992)
8. Thornly Park Student Village. Not shown (1993-96)
9. E Block South (1993)
10. Oswald Buildings (1994)
11. Emery Residences, Christie Street. Not shown (1995)
12. Thornly Park Sports Centre. Not shown (1995)
13. Scottish Property Network not shown (1996)
14. Library and Learning Resource Centre under construction (1998)
15. Planned Buildings
16. Goods Despatch / Security (1993)

In this period also, the Lady Lane Residences (17) and George Street flats (18) were refurbished as were the Wellmeadow (19) and School Wynd Lecture halls (not shown). The Weighhouse Close and Shuttle Street halls were demolished.

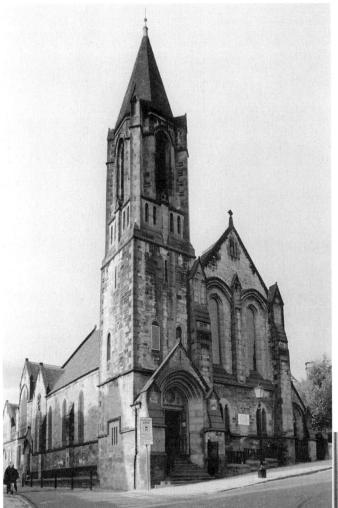

School Wynd Lecture Halls (formerly the School Wynd Church)

BOTTOM LEFT: Wellmeadow Lecture Halls (formerly the Elim Church)

Adam Ls Lynch, Director of Estates and Buildings completes thirty years service in 1997. For most of this time he has been the driving force behind the transformation of the Paisley Campus and adjacent town centre buildings. The department now has over 180 employees.

Emery Residences
in Christie Street,
opened in 1995.

The opening of
Thornly Park
Sports Centre.

Scotland football
Manager and
former Craigie
Lecturer Craig
Brown at the
opening of the
Thornly Park
Sports Centre.

Paisley People

Janitorial staff. From left to right, back row: Frank Morrow, Dave McInally, Tom McFarlane, Bill Gilchrist, John Patton, Greg Boyle, Pat McAteer. Front row: George Connell, George McOnnichie, Irvin Allen.

LEFT: Former Vice-Principal Woodward.

RIGHT: Professor G. Findlay, Department of Mechanical Engineering.

LEFT: Professor Willey.

RIGHT: David Rigg, University Registrar.

Chapter 9
Forward by Degrees

The University's story forms a pattern of overlapping circles. Once, Paisley Abbey held sway over a large part of south-west Scotland; now the University covers much the same area. It is fitting that when town and gown (Renfrew District Provost William Orr and Principal Richard Shaw) took part in the District's official welcome to the new University, they met in Paisley Abbey.

In the fifteenth century the lands of Craigie in Ayrshire, including the daughter-church of Craigie, were gifted to Paisley Abbey; and in the early 1990s Craigie College in Ayrshire became the new University's second campus. One hundred years ago the Coats family, wealthy Paisley benefactors, donated the parcel of land that Paisley Technical School was first built on; now graduates of the University which grew from the school are capped in the Thomas Coats Memorial Baptist Church.

At the end of the nineteenth century, one of the Brough Trustees urged his colleagues to encourage the new Technical School to work in partnership with local industry, and in 1913 a similar suggestion was made by a staff member. Both men were snubbed at the time, but today their foresight is reflected in the very strong bonds between the University and industry, both local and widespread.

Although engineering is no longer one of the area's main industries, the University of Paisley continues to emphasise the need for top-class courses for its engineering students. In February 1996 a state-of-the-art laboratory for the study of materials science was formally opened on-campus, the result of a joint venture between the University and U.S.-based firm Buehler-Krautkramer plc, an international specialist in materials science. One of at least four state-of-the-art laboratories established on-campus by international specialist companies over the years, it gives engineering students access to one of the most advanced laboratories of its kind in the UK.

At the end of the nineteenth century, the sudden realisation that Europe was outstripping Britain in technology led to the formation of institutions such as Paisley Technical School. In the 1980s a similar realisation, this time concerning micro-electronics, led to the formation of MEDC (the Micro-Electronic Educational Development Centre) at Paisley.

The world-famous Paisley Pattern is echoed in the university's academic dress, and even the University itself has turned about, in a half-circle at least, to front onto the High Street instead of George Street.

Success Stories

Dr Bill Elder.

Dr Bill Elder, who attended Paisley College of Technology on day release and evening classes while employed by Rootes as a work study engineer, moved to America where, on St Andrew's Day 1981, he started his own company, Genus, now a world leader in thin film technology. Bill returned to Paisley in 1994 to speak at the University about his success, and again in 1995 to receive the honorary degree of Doctor of the University (DUniv). In 1996 he set up an annual foundation prize, aimed at assisting students who share his own 'can do' policy to set up their own businesses.

M.E.Ps Ken Collins and Bill Millar both attended Paisley College of Technology, Ken Collins as a lecturer and Bill Millar as a student, while Graham Watson, the Liberal Democrats' first M.E.P., worked in Registry during the 1980s. Rugby internationalist Gavin Hastings graduated with an Honours degree from the Land Economics Department in the mid-1980s, and went

Gavin Hastings receives an Honorary Degree.

on to take his Master's at Cambridge before becoming captain of Scotland's rugby team, then moving to American football as a member of the Scottish Claymores.

Many other former students scattered to the four corners of the earth have enjoyed successful careers in a wide variety of occupations.

Evening Classes

Having started with evening-classes, the University is again, at the close of its first century, turning full circle with a return to evening studies. Credit Accumulation Transfer Scheme (CATS) classes, including post-graduate courses, have become popular with students who, because of work or other commitments, find it convenient to study in the evenings and on Saturday mornings.

Principal Shaw sees these classes, which, he points out, are more flexible than they used to be, as one of the most important moves in higher education, opening up opportunities to people who were unable to gain qualifications in their earlier years.

'Evening-class graduations are a pleasure,' he says, 'and very often they are family occasions too.' University Librarian Stuart James agrees. 'Our lecturers used to say at graduations, "I taught his or her mother or father." Now they say, "I taught his or her granddaughter or grandson."'

Higher Education Problems

Sadly, as the world grows smaller and education opportunities increase, life for Britain's higher education students grows more precarious. A trust fund set up in 1992 to mark the university's inauguration and help students in need, came into such demand in 1995 that it almost ran out of money. It was saved by a £21,000 donation by Renfrew District Council to mark its 21st year in office. In 1996, under local reorganisation, the District Council itself came to an end.

As has been said earlier, the search among universities for students to fill their lecture rooms and laboratories now stretches across the world market, while our own students struggle to fund their higher education.

Principals

The School/College/University has been well-served by its seven Principals, with each moving it a step forward. Angus McLean established its high standard of education, and brought in London External Degree work, while Lewis Fry Richardson introduced the HND and HNC courses and paved the way for day-release students.

John Denholm welcomed the influx of Babcock trainees which helped to establish the College and resulted in a similar ICI apprenticeship scheme.

Hugh Henry put an end to the localised and at times claustrophobic relationships which had begun to hold the institution back.

Edwin Kerr presided over the introduction of CNAA courses and began to prepare the College for University status.

Tom Howie developed many of the departments and introduced the Nepal project, which led to other activities world-wide, and during the final eleven years of the institution's first century Principal Richard Shaw, building on the steady progress made by his predecessors, has overseen the move from Paisley College of Technology into a two-campus University geared to meet industrial and technological needs not only within its own area, but on a world-wide basis.

Staff

Throughout its progress from School to College to University, the institution has been blessed with staff totally committed to its development. Some names have come to the fore through the pages of this history, but they are only a few of the people who have contributed to the University's success.

Survival and Growth

Throughout the twentieth century, Paisley's higher education institution has been buffeted by wars, industrial depressions, problems of finance and space, and political and technological changes. At times its very existence has been in danger, but despite everything it has survived.

If draper Peter Brough were to stroll down Paisley High Street today, in his navy blue frock coat, black vest and trousers, and high shirt collar 'stiffly starched and covering the full half of his cheek,' he would surely be startled to see what had grown from the bequests left in his will. Startled, but also pleased, in his quiet way

Paisley University's Alumni Magazine, *The Eye*, takes its name from a comment made in a novel by nineteenth century Prime Minister Benjamin Disraeli. As far as the University is concerned, the words are as apt today as they were then, 'Keep your eye on Paisley.'

References

The sources of specific references mentioned in the text are listed below by chapter, page and paragraph. The principal sources are listed in the bibliography.

Chapter 1

Page 15, para	3,	Sturrock, p51 and 52.
17	4	Education Act 1872
18	7	Bell, p131
19	3	*Scots Pictorial*, 15th January 1900, p21
19	8	*Paisley and Renfrewshire Gazette*, 28th April 1906, p5
20	2	Samuelson Report as quoted in Graham, p47
21	7	Technical Schools (Scotland) Act 1886
27	3	*Lady's Pictorial*, 11th December 1897, p877
27	3	*Paisley and Renfrewshire Gazette*, 4th December 1897, p5
28	2	*Education News*, 4th December 1897, p825

Chapter 2

32	1	*Paisley Technical School Calendar* 1899-1900, p12
33	5	Murphy, p268
36	2	*Empire Exhibition Scotland, 1938, Official Guide*, p107
37	1	Code of Regulations for Continuation Classes, 1901
38	7	Graham, p111
42	2	*UK Technical and Art Schools and Colleges Handbook* London, Scott, Greenwood and Son, 1909, p103
42	5	Graham, p118
44	2	Graham, p266
45	5	Education (Scotland) Act 1918
49	5	*Paisley and Renfrewshire Gazette*, 1st May 1926, p5
49	6	Mitchell, p4
50	4	Graham, p128
50	5	Percy Report, as discussed in Graham, p123

Chapter 3

52	6	Ashford, p142
53	4	National Economy Act 1931
56	2	Graham, p153
57	1	Education (Scotland) Paisley Technical College and School of Art Special Grant Regulations 1938
59	7	Ashford, p168
60	1	Richardson (1935)

60	1	Richardson (1939)
60	4	*Dictionary of National Bibliography*, 1951-60, p837-9
63	1	Richardson (1993)
63	7	Graham, p160-161
64	4	*Guardian*, 9th April 1993, p22

Chapter 4

| 68 | 4 | *Impact*, No. 6, 3rd December 1968, p4 |

Chapter 5

78	5	Report on Technical Education, 1946
78	6	Education (Scotland) Act 1946
78	6	Central Institutions (Scotland) Act 1947
83	2	Paisley Technical College Scheme 1954
93	6	White Paper 1956
98	2	Toothill Report as discussed in Graham, p277
103	2	Robbins Report, as discussed in Graham, p206 onwards

Chapter 6

114	6	Mitchell, p4
115	6	Wilson, p2
121	4	Graham, p283
125	5	*Impact*, No. 6, 3rd December 1968, p1
128	2	*Impact*, No. 9, March 1969, p3
133	8	*Impact*, No. 6, 3rd December 1968, p4
134	1	Robbins Report, as discussed in Graham, p206 onwards

Chapter 7

141	5	Rochester Report, as discussed in Graham, p237
143	3	Bolton Report, as discussed in Graham, p234
151	1	Jack, p30
153	2	Marshall, *Proceedings of the International Conference on Composite Structures*
153	2	Marshall, *Composite Structures*

Chapter 8

162	6	White Paper 1991
163	4	*Executive Report*, Term 3, No. 1, (c.1991)
182	1	*Danson*, Millar and Reeves (1996)

Chapter 9

| 190 | 5 | Disraeli. According to Paisley historian David Rowand a quote from *Endymion* (London, Longman, 1880) |

Bibliography

1. Principal Sources

Academic Board Minutes.	Paisley College of Technology
Annual Reports.	Paisley College of Technology
Board of Governors Minutes.	Paisley College of Technology
Calendar	Paisley College of Technology
Centenary Oral History Project	University of Paisley Library
Graham, David S.	*The Origins and Development of Paisley College of Technology from 1895 to 1980.* Unpublished PhD Thesis. Paisley, Paisley College of Technology, 1990.
McDowall, David	*Technical Education in Paisley 1870-1920.* Unpublished M.Ed Thesis. Glasgow, Glasgow University, 1972
Prospectuses	Paisley College of Technology/University of Paisley

2. Other University Records and Publications

Danson, Mike; Millar, Chris and Reeves, Alan	*Impact of the University of Paisley: a study of the University in its wider economic and physical environment in the counties of Ayrshire and Renfrewshire.* Paisley, Department of Economics and Management, University of Paisley, 1996
The Eye	University of Paisley Alumni Magazine, 1991 onwards
Impact	Paisley College of Technology Students' Magazine c.1968-70
Jack, James Cunningham	*The College Poems 1939-1989* Paisley, Paisley Tech Press, 1989
Mitchell, Alastair D	*90 Years of Degree Teaching in Chemistry.* Paisley, Paisley College Department of Chemistry and Chemical Engineering, 1991

Student Newsletters   Various titles, held in Library archive

Wilson, Alan G   *The Computer Centre: The First 25 Years.* Paisley, University of Paisley Computer Centre, 1992

3. *Government Publications*

Central Institutions (Scotland) Act 1947

Code of Regulations for Continuation Classes, 1901

Education Act 1872

Education (Scotland) Act 1918

Education (Scotland) Act 1946

Education (Scotland) Paisley Technical College and School of Art Special Grant Regulation 1938

Higher Education: A New Framework. DES, Scottish Office, Northern Ireland Office and Welsh Office (White Paper)

National Economy Act 1931

Paisley Technical College Scheme 1954

Report of the Committee on Education and Industry, London, HMSO 1928 (Percy Report)

Report of the Committee on Education and Industry in Scotland, Edinburgh, HMSO 1928

Report of the Committee on Higher Education London, HMSO 1963 (Robbins Report)

Report on Technical Education, Advisory Council for Education in Scotland. Edinburgh, HMSO, 1946

Role of Small Firms in the National Economy London, HMSO 1971 (Bolton Report)

Royal Commission on Technical Instruction. 1884 (Samuelson Report)

Technical Education Act 1956

Technical Schools (Scotland) Act 1887

4. *Other Reports*

Resources for Research in Polytechnics and Other Institutions, the Report of a Working Party of the CNAA London, CNAA 1970 (Rochester Report)

Inquiry into the Scottish Economy. Edinburgh, Scottish Council (Development and Industry), 1961 (Toothill Report)

5. *Periodicals and Magazines*

Education News

GESA (The magazine of Babcock and Wilcox Graduates and Students' Association)

Guardian

Herald

Composite Structures published by Elsevier/Applied Science

Lady's Pictorial

Nobel Times (The newspaper of ICI Nobel Division)

Paisley and Renfrewshire Gazette
Paisley Daily Express
Scots Pictorial

6. Secondary Sources

Ashford, Oliver M	*Prophet or Professor? The Life and Work of Lewis Fry Richardson.* Bristol, Hilger 1985
Bell, Quentin	*The Schools of Design.* London, Routledge and Kogan Page 1963
Blair, Matthew	*The Paisley Thread Industry.* Paisley, Alexander Gardner 1907
Carter, Jennifer J and Withrington, Donald J (eds)	*Scottish Universities: Distinctiveness and Diversity.* Edinburgh, John Donald 1992
Clark, Sylvia	*Paisley, A History.* Edinburgh Mainstream 1988

Empire Exhibition Scotland; Official Guide 1938

Marshall, I H (Ed)	*Proceedings of the International Conferences on Composite Structures 8.* London, Elsevier/ Applied Science, 1981 onwards
Fraser, W Hamish and Morris, R J (eds)	*People and Society in Scotland Vol. 2, 1830-1914.* Edinburgh, John Donald 1990
Murphy, William S	*Captains of Industry.* Glasgow, W S Murphy, 1901
Richardson, Lewis Fry	*The Collected Papers of Lewis Fry Richardson.* 2 vols. Cambridge, Cambridge University Press, 1993
Richardson, Lewis Fry	*Generalised Foreign Politics: A Study in Group Psychology.* Cambridge, Cambridge University 1934
Richardson, Lewis Fry	'Mathematical Psychology of War' in *Nature* Vol. 135 1935, p830-1
Venables, Peter	*Higher Educational Developments: The Technological Universities.* London, Faber and Faber, 1978
Williams, E T and Palmer, Helen M	*Dictionary of National Biography*, 1951-60. Oxford, Oxford University Press, 1971

Index